Teaching Problem Solving Through Children's Literature

Teaching Problem Solving Through Children's Literature

James W. Forgan, Ph.D.

Florida Atlantic University

Illustrated by

David Tripp

2003
Teacher Ideas Press
Libraries Unlimited
A Division of Greenwood Publishing Group, Inc.
Westport, Connecticut

TEACHER IDEAS PRESS
Libraries Unlimited
A Division of Greenwood Publishing Group, Inc.
88 Post Road West
Westport, CT 06881
1-800-225-5800
www.lu.com/tips

ISBN 1-56308-981-5

This book is dedicated to my wonderful wife, Peggy, and my loving children, Emily and Teddy. Thank you for helping me to become a better problem solver! Special thanks also go to the fantastic teachers in the Martin County School District in Stuart, Florida, who allowed me to try these activities with their students.

Contents

List of Figures

Introduction to Problem Solving

How to Use This Book

This book is designed as a tool for teachers, counselors, and others working with elementary-age children to use as one component of a proactive instructional classroom management plan that emphasizes active problem solving and appropriate social skills. It is organized into nine chapters, with the first chapter explaining the key components of problem solving using children's literature and providing an introduction to these concepts. The following eight chapters contain lesson plans on issues such as bullying, self-concept, friendship, and dealing with differences. Each chapter contains five lesson plans using current children's literature books. In each chapter, all lesson plans are grouped by topic, but many lessons contain subtopics, because issues often overlap. For example, one lesson's primary focus may be on friendship and its secondary focus on responding to teasing.

These lessons are designed for teachers to easily integrate into the literacy or affective curriculum of the typical school day. It is preferable to discuss and teach these important topics within a natural learning context involving reading and writing (Cartledge and Milburn 1995). Teaching in the natural context is important for two primary reasons. First, from the teacher's viewpoint, creating a separate time to discuss social issues is difficult when schools are often pressured with increasing academic test scores. Second, students generalize and maintain the information more easily when problem solving is learned within reading and writing activities rather than practiced in isolation.

Additionally, the lessons in this book promote cooperation and shared problem solving because each lesson plan contains a format that promotes guided discussions and reinforcement activities. Each lesson contains 10 suggested questions for teachers to use during guided discussions. These questions do not create an exhaustive list but are samples to help teachers begin class discussions. Teachers are encouraged to create their own questions to match the interests of their students. There is one problem-solving practice scenario and one reproducible reinforcement activity for each lesson in the book. Again, these are suggested to complement the children's literature story. Many of the lesson activities can be interchanged. Students sometimes suggest follow-up activities that may complement the lesson or may be useful for a future lesson.

After using the first lesson plan, instructors should focus on teaching students in grade one and above the I SOLVE interpersonal problem-solving strategy for identifying their problematic issue and examining potential solutions for solving the issue. Once taught, practiced, and mastered, students can apply this strategy to any difficulty they experience within their school environment or community.

Introduction to Problem Solving in the Classroom

Using Children's Literature to Teach Problem Solving

Have you ever read a book for self-help or to find answers to your difficulties, such as how others overcame financial woes, learned to become self-confident, or turned professional failure into success? If you answered yes, then you have used the principles of problem solving as related to literature. At one time or another, most people have read a book to determine how others approached a delicate issue. Examples of books adults might read are *The Seven Habits of Highly Effective People* by Steven R. Covey or *How to Talk to Anyone, Anytime, Anywhere* by Larry King and B. Gilbert. Teachers can use children's literature books to help students solve problems and generate appropriate alternate responses to their issues.

Using books to solve problems has received increased attention in recent years. Aiex (1993) identified nine possible reasons a teacher may choose to use children's literature to teach problem solving with students:

1. To show an individual that he or she is not the first or only person to encounter such a problem

2. To show an individual that there is more than one solution to a problem

3. To help a person discuss a problem more freely

4. To help an individual plan a constructive course of action to solve a problem

5. To develop an individual's self-concept

6. To relieve emotional or mental pressure

7. To foster an individual's honest self-appraisal

8. To provide a way for a person to find interests outside of self

9. To increase an individual's understanding of human behavior or motivations

This list is not exhaustive but highlights some of the many potential benefits to using children's literature to teach students problem solving. Once you have taught your students how to solve problems, this should help improve the classroom climate and reduce some of the minor issues requiring teacher assistance to solve. By teaching students the steps of problem solving, you become proactive and empower students.

Students in both general and special education will benefit from developing problem-solving skills (McCarty and Chalmers 1997) because they may be experiencing difficulties at the moment or in the future. For example, just because a student may not be confronted by a bully or teased this week does not mean he or she will never experience these problems. Participating in the children's literature lessons helps students develop empathy for classmates who may be experiencing difficulty. Students who learn and apply the principles from these lessons can become proficient problem solvers who respond constructively when confronted with problematic situations.

The situations most teachers explore with students are everyday life problems and issues such as diversity, anger, teasing, and bullying. This type of problem solving is best accomplished through small group or whole class readings and discussions of the topic. The ready-to-use lesson plans in this book are based on an instructional teaching and problem-solving framework and contain the four stages of prereading, guided reading, postreading discussion, and extended learning activities. All extended learning activities include role plays as well as an activity. Each component is explained in the section "Problem-Solving Practice Scenario."

Through the process of teaching problem solving using children's literature, your students will pass through the stages of identification, catharsis, and resolution as they learn to solve problems. Doll and Doll (1997) believe this is an important process and one in which "problem solving provided by literature will cause young people to change the ways in which they interact with or behave toward other people." By identifying with the literary character, students recognize they are not alone in experiencing a problem. This is important, as young people often feel they are the only one experiencing a specific problem. When students feel a sense of belonging and a connection with the teacher and other classmates, they help create a positive learning climate.

Through the guided class discussion of the character's problem, students can discuss the issue and realize that other people experience the same problems. This dialogue helps students develop insight into the character's difficulty as they discuss the merits and shortcomings of any solutions. Then, as a class, students can generate possible solutions to their own problems by using a mnemonic strategy.

Steps for Teaching Problem Solving

Often elementary students believe that the teacher must solve all problems because they have not learned to become independent problem solvers. By participating in these lessons, students will learn how to become independent problem solvers. They can apply the I SOLVE interpersonal problem-solving strategy to develop additional alternatives for solving problems. Once students become efficient problem solvers, they develop feelings of self-control, which are important for creating a positive classroom environment (Dreikurs and Cassel 1972).

The postreading follow-up section for each lesson plan includes application of the I SOLVE mnemonic strategy. The steps of I SOLVE are as follows:

I: Identify the problem presented in the book.

S: Solutions to the problem are brainstormed.

O: Obstacles to the solutions are identified.

L: Look at the solutions again and choose one.

V: Validate the solution by trying it.

E: Evaluate how the solution worked.

Let's examine each one of the steps independently, although each step is interrelated (see fig. 1.1 for a reproducible copy). Step 1: *Identify* the problem presented in the book. You may find that there are several problems presented in the book that seem relevant to your students. It may be necessary to guide students to the primary issue for your discussion and then address secondary problems during another lesson.

Step 2: Brainstorm *solutions* to the problem. Students list all solutions the book's characters considered to solve the problem as well as generate their own original solutions to the problem. Instruct students to generate numerous potential solutions, because a solution may appear promising but not work when closely considered. It is helpful to write the potential solutions on the chalkboard or overhead projector to facilitate their discussion because the next step involves writing the obstacles to each solution. The transparency master found in figure 1.2 may be reproduced to record potential solutions and obstacles the children identify.

Step 3: Identify *obstacles* to the solutions. Explore each solution to determine any obstacles or unpleasant consequences that might eliminate this solution. Write the obstacles adjacent to the solutions.

I   Identify the Problem.

S   Solutions to the Problem?

O   Obstacles to the Solutions?

L   Look at the Solutions Again—

Choose One.

V   Validate the Solution by Trying It.

E   Evaluate how the Solution Worked.

Figure 1. I SOLVE Strategy

The I SOLVE steps are:

I: Identify the problem presented in the book.

S: Solutions to the problem are brainstormed.

O: Obstacles to the solution are identified.

L: Look at the solutions again and choose one.

V: Validate the solution by trying it.

E: Evaluate how the solution worked.

Identify problem: _____

Solutions: 1. _____

2. _____

3. _____

Obstacles: 1. _____

2. _____

3. _____

Look and choose: _____

Validate by trying it:

1. Which one will you try? _____

Evaluate the outcome:

1. Did it work? _____

Figure 2. Transparency Master

Reassure students that it is typical for many of the solutions to have obstacles. They should try to determine a solution with few or no obstacles that effectively solves the problem.

Step 4: *Look* at the solutions again and choose one. Emphasize to students that they need to select solutions that provide long-term solutions. This may mean eliminating some attractive but short-term or temporary solutions. Remind students to make sure they do not just choose the solution with the least obstacles, as it may not always solve the problem.

Step 5: *Validate* the solution by trying it. Explain to students that the term *validate* means to test or try something. The next time students have a problem, they should validate or test the new solution and see how it solves the problem. In this book, the problem-solving practice scenarios and some reinforcement activities include role plays to provide students with immediate practice. Students may need prompting to try the new solution until applying the I SOLVE strategy becomes automatic.

Step 6: *Evaluate* the solution to determine if it was effective at helping to solve the problem. Initially students may need guidance from the teacher to help evaluate if the problem was effectively solved. This type of teacher-provided scaffolding is important until the students gradually take responsibility for evaluating their actions. If the solution was ineffective, the student would need to return to the **S** step and reconsider the remaining solutions.

Teaching the I SOLVE Strategy

Strategy instruction has four components: *providing a rationale*, *teacher modeling*, *guided practice*, and *skill maintenance and generalization* to new settings.

Component 1: Each time you introduce the I SOLVE strategy, provide the rationale for why it is important to learn how to solve problems. Begin by asking students if they have ever experienced problems with their friends or classmates. Ask a volunteer to share their problem, or share one of your personal experiences with a problem. After sharing, emphasize to students that you are going to teach them a strategy to help them solve these types of problems. Tell them the strategy is called "I SOLVE" because it emphasizes working together to solve problems. Let the students know you are going to begin teaching the strategy and continue practicing it until they can apply it independently. Remember that students will not master a new strategy in one, two, or even three lessons.

Component 2: Model the steps of the I SOLVE interpersonal problem-solving strategy to the students. Reproduce figure 1.1 and provide each student with a copy, or enlarge the I SOLVE steps and post them in a visible location. Begin by telling students that I SOLVE is an acronym and that each letter in I SOLVE stands for a different step in helping to solve problems. Read each letter and the statement it represents from the display chart.

An I SOLVE Example

Using an example of a problem, model the second strategy instructional component of applying the steps of I SOLVE and write them on the chalkboard or overhead projector (see fig. 1.2). For example, as the teacher I would model the strategy by sharing a common elementary school experience such as losing a pencil or forgetting a homework assignment. For example, one day I was driving my seven-year-old daughter, Emily, to school when she remembered that she forgot her notebook. Emily was worried because she was supposed to turn in her homework assignment. This is a realistic example to use when illustrating the I SOLVE strategy.

First, ***identify*** (stress this word while pointing to the step on the chart) the problem. Model the strategy steps and "think aloud" so that students hear the metacognitive process of thinking about our own thinking. In my situation I identified the problem: My daughter did not have her homework to turn in.

Next, brainstorm a list of possible *solutions* to the problem (each time you move to another step, stress and point to the step). These were some possible solutions to the problem:

◆ We return to the house to retrieve the homework assignment.

◆ Emily doesn't turn in the assignment.

◆ Emily explains the situation to her teacher and asks if she could turn in the assignment the next day.

Let students know it is permissible to generate a longer list of potential solutions. The purpose of the brainstorm is to help students to think about many different ways for solving the problem.

Next, tell students that *obstacles* are like barriers or roadblocks that may stop them from successfully solving the problem. Some solutions first appear wonderful but upon closer examination have a barrier that makes them unattractive. These were the obstacles to my three potential solutions:

◆ Returning home would have made Emily late for school, because this would have delayed us an additional 20 minutes. Returning home would have also made me late for work.

◆ Not turning in the assignment would have resulted in Emily receiving an F grade, and she would have felt bad about the situation.

◆ Explaining the situation to her teacher might have caused the teacher to say, "No, you cannot turn the assignment in late."

Step three is to *look* again at all the solutions and obstacles and think about which solution is associated with the least negative consequences and can help to solve the problem for the long term. Again "think aloud" and examine each solution and obstacle. We selected the third solution: Emily would talk to her teacher.

The next step, *validate by trying it*, required Emily to talk to her teacher once she arrived at school. Emily discussed the problem with her teacher, and her teacher was very understanding.

In the final step, *evaluate how the solution worked*, I tell students that the teacher allowed Emily to turn her homework in the next day, since she rarely forgets it. I explain to students that if the outcome had not been successful, I would return to the *look* step and choose another solution to try.

Component 3: Provide *practice* for students to apply the I SOLVE steps. Teachers can ask for additional examples of problems and have students model the I SOLVE steps in front of the class as they provide guidance. Another activity is to provide a generic problem for all students to solve (such as what to do when they need a snack or when they do not understand an assignment), divide the class into groups, and let them practice the steps. As students work in groups, circulate throughout the room and provide feedback. Once students finish, ask a group to role-play the I SOLVE strategy for the class. In each lesson plan in this book, the I SOLVE strategy and problem-solving practice scenario provide students opportunities for practicing the strategy.

Component 4: Help students *maintain* this strategy as well as *generalize* this strategy to other school or community settings. As discussed prior, after your initial instruction, students need prompting and guidance to remember when to apply the I SOLVE strategy. As the classroom teacher, use the "teachable moment" to remind and guide students. Daily opportunities arise for students to practice problem solving in the classroom and on the playground. By applying and using the problem-solving strategy, students will remember the strategy. Some teachers find that assigning strategy homework helps students remember to use the problem-solving strategy in other contexts. Give students a homework checklist (see fig. 1.3) to complete, which documents using the I SOLVE strategy.

In sum, strategy instruction is valuable and effective for giving students a tool for solving their own problems.

Name: _____   Date: _____

I'm a Problem Solver!

Directions: Make a check mark to show you used I SOLVE, and circle the face that shows how you did with each problem-solving step.

Remember the I SOLVE steps:

I: Identify the problem.

S: Solutions to the problem are brainstormed.

O: Obstacles to the solutions are identified.

L: Look at the solutions again and choose one.

V: Validate the solution by trying it.

E: Evaluate how the solution worked.

_____ I used I SOLVE.

Circle the face that shows how you did.

Identify the problem.	☺	😐	☹
Solutions?	☺	😐	☹
Obstacles?	☺	😐	☹
Look and choose.	☺	😐	☹
Try it!	☺	😐	☹
Evaluate.	☺	😐	☹

Parent or Teacher comments: _____

_____

Figure 3. Homework Checklist

Problem-Solving Instructional Framework

The lessons in this book are based on a literacy instructional framework for problem solving and contain the four stages of *prereading*, *guided reading*, *postreading discussion*, and *extended learning activities*. Each stage is elaborated next.

The first stage of *prereading* relates to selecting materials and activating student knowledge. Careful selection of material is important so that students can identify and relate to the literature character, either real or fictional. Lessons from this book are already developed, but teachers can develop additional lessons using their favorite children's literature books. The school or public library media specialist is usually a knowledgeable source for recommending books that parents discuss with their children. Internet sites also provide synopses of books. One Internet site is the Carnegie Library of Pittsburgh. This web site has very detailed summaries of books to help young children cope in today's world. The web address is www.clpgh.org/clp/libctr/famctr/bibtherapy.

Activating students' background knowledge helps them connect their past experiences to the present content of the book. Often teachers display the cover of the book and ask students to predict what occurs in the story. Others provide a brief statement about the story and ask students a question such as, "The story we are going to read today is about bullies. Have you ever been bothered by a bully?" Teachers may want to use a Venn diagram to allow students to predict some of the similarities and differences between their lives and the characters in the book. These types of predicting activities help students bring their personal experiences forefront and assist with helping students identify with the book's topic.

Guided reading is the second stage of the teaching framework and involves the teacher or adult reading the story aloud. Generally children's literature books are of reasonable length to completely read during one class period, although some chapter books require multiple reading sessions. During reading, pause just prior to the point where the main character solves the problem. At this point you can ask the students to predict how they think the character will solve the problem. Students can also apply the steps of I SOLVE to generate additional solutions to the problem. Once you have worked through the I SOLVE strategy, continue reading and see if the students' predictions were correct.

After the story is completed, some teachers allow the students a few minutes to write down their reaction to the story in a literature journal. Others simply allow a few seconds for individual reflection on the story before beginning the discussion. Some teachers prefer to segment their reading to make comments or point out similarities between the book's characters and their students; this format is fine, too.

The third stage of the teaching framework is the *postreading discussion*. McCarty and Chalmers (1997) provide guidelines for the discussion and recommend that the teacher first have students retell the plot, then evaluate character feelings and any situations that occurred. This is followed by a class discussion when "the students are asked probing questions, which helps them think about their feelings and better identify with the characters and events in the story." The discussion section for each lesson in this book contains 10 questions teachers can use to stimulate a meaningful class discussion. The questions vary in terms of Bloom's taxonomy in that some are knowledge and comprehension questions, whereas others require analysis and evaluation.

During the guided discussion, refer students to the character's solution and the alternate solutions the class generated using the I SOLVE strategy. Ask students how they would have reacted if the character's problem-solving solution did not work. Which of the remaining class solutions are viable options for solving the problem? During the discussion continue to "think aloud" so students see the pros and cons as well as related consequences of each solution. Thinking aloud helps students learn to complete this process themselves.

The final stage of the teaching framework includes the *extended learning activities*. The extended learning activities include one role-playing section titled "Problem-Solving Practice Scenario" and one reproducible reinforcement activity. The problem-solving practice scenarios are intended to provide students with an opportunity to actively participate in practicing the I SOLVE strategy. These scenarios are situations students may encounter in school and within their communities. Vary group composition as students practice role playing. After students role-play and discuss the problem, provide feedback on their performance.

All lessons contain a reproducible reinforcement activity that incorporates literacy activities such as writing, poetry, artwork, or games. The reinforcement activities are used after the lesson is taught to provide students with extra practice needed to reinforce the skill. These activities allow students to gain additional practice in a nonthreatening manner. Many of these reproducible activities can also be assigned as homework.

Summary Suggestions for Using the Lesson Plans

Remember to consider the following questions when selecting and using each lesson plan:

♦ Does the lesson plan objective match the needs of my students?

♦ Are the needed materials easily accessible?

♦ Do the prereading activities need modifications?

♦ Which guided questions sound the most appropriate for my students?

♦ Will students be successful with the I SOLVE problem-solving strategy?

♦ Is the reinforcement activity at the appropriate instructional level for my students, or do I need to make modifications?

♦ Am I going to give students homework to accompany the lesson?

Considering these questions before initiating instruction will help the lesson flow smoothly.

References

Aiex, N. K. 1993. *Bibliotherapy.* Report No. EDO-CS-93-05. Bloomington, Ind.: Indiana University, Office of Educational Research and Improvement. ERIC Document Reproduction Service No. ED 357 333.

Cartledge, G., and J. F. Milburn. 1995. *Teaching social skills to children and youth: Innovative approaches.* 3d ed. Boston: Allyn & Bacon.

Cosby, B. 1997. *The meanest thing to say.* New York: Scholastic.

Covey, S. R. 1989. *The seven habits of highly effective people: Restoring the character ethic.* New York: Simon & Schuster.

Doll, B., and C. Doll. 1997. *Bibliotherapy with young people: Librarians and mental health professionals working together.* Englewood, Colo.: Libraries Unlimited.

Dreikurs, R., and P. Cassel. 1972. *Discipline without tears.* New York: Hawthorn.

King, L., and B. Gilbert. 1994. *How to talk to anyone, anytime, anywhere: The secrets of good communication.* New York: Crown Publishers.

McCarty, H., and L. Chalmers. 1997. *Bibliotherapy intervention and prevention: Teaching exceptional children*, 12–17.

Helping Students Respond to Bullies

Each lesson in this chapter helps students develop appropriate responses to bullies and teasing. Most students, at one time or another, are teased. Persistent teasing can lead a student to develop unpleasant feelings toward school. All lessons in this chapter help students learn strategies for appropriately responding to bullies.

The Meanest Thing to Say

Title: *The Meanest Thing to Say*
Author: Bill Cosby
Illustrator: Varnette P. Honeywood
Copyright: 1997
Publisher: Scholastic
ISBN: 0-590-13754-9
Topic: Responding to teasing
Approximate Grade Levels: K–3

Book Summary:
>   A new boy joins Little Bill's class and wants to play a name-calling game. Little Bill has to choose between saying mean things or coming up with another solution. With the help of his family, Little Bill responds to the confrontation at school by saying "So?" and refusing to participate. The mean boy leaves in embarrassment, feeling insecure and lonely. Empathizing with the new boy, Little Bill befriends him.

Lesson Goals:
>   To help students select strategies to effectively deal with name-calling and bullies. To help students realize students who pick on others are often insecure.

Prereading Activities:

Ask students if they have ever been called mean names. Follow up by asking them to share how they felt when called mean names. Summarize by saying it hurts our feelings and does not make people feel good when they are called names. Tell the students you will read them a book about what happened to a boy named Little Bill when a new student in his class started calling him names. Read students the book title and ask them to make predictions about the story.

During Reading:

Read the story aloud. At the end, allow students time for individual reflection.

Postreading/Discussion Questions:

After reading the story, go through it again with students and ask questions such as the following:

1. What could the other kids have said when Michael wanted to start "playing the dozens"?

2. How did Little Bill feel when Michael left the playground and said, "Tomorrow!"?

3. Why was Little Bill so mad that he could not think of any mean things to say to Michael?

4. How do you think Little Bill's friends were feeling when he was saying "So?" to Michael? Did they support him?

5. What do you think would have happened to Little Bill if he went to school and said mean things to Michael?

6. How was Michael feeling when he ran inside the classroom? Why?

7. Who else could you talk to about this type of problem?

8. Why would Little Bill feel sorry for Michael when Michael was going to say mean things to him?

9. What would you do if you were Little Bill and saw Michael sitting at his desk?

10. What should you do if you are in a similar situation?

I SOLVE Strategy

I: Identify the problem presented in the book.

➤ Little Bill is challenged to play a game to call people mean names.

S: Solutions to the problem?

   a. Book suggestion: Little Bill's dad tells him to say "So?" when someone calls him a name.

   b. Ignore him and walk away.

   c. Call him a mean name.

   d. Other:

O: Obstacles to the solutions?

    a.   Book suggestion: Michael may continue to call Little Bill names.

    b.   Ignoring him may not be effective.

    c.   Calling him mean names may lead to more troubles.

    d.   Other:

L: Look at the solutions again and choose one.
Select the strategy you feel would work best.

V: Validate the solution by trying it.

E: Evaluate how the solution worked.

    Was it successful? If not, return to step **S** for additional solutions.

Extended Learning Activities

1. Problem-Solving Practice Scenario

> Imagine you have an older brother. Your older brother teases you by calling you names because he likes to see you get mad. His favorite names for you are midget and shortie. Usually you tell your mom when he calls you a name. What else could you do?

I: Identify the problem.

    ➤ The older brother teases you by name-calling.

S: Solutions to the problem?

    a.   Run away from brother.

    b.   Call him names.

    c.   Ignore him by pretending he is invisible.

    d.   Other:

O: Obstacles to the solutions?

    a.   If you run away, he may follow.

    b.   If you call him names, he may just laugh.

    c.   If you ignore him and pretend he is invisible, he may go away.

    d.   Other:

L: Look at the solutions again and choose one.

Suggest that students may want to try letter **c** first because if the brother does not see you get mad, he may stop teasing.

V: Validate the solution by trying it.

Tell students they would try the solution and see how brother acted.

E: Evaluate how the solution worked.

If brother stopped teasing you, then the problem is solved. If he still teases you, return to step **S** and brainstorm new solutions as well as review the old solutions. Continue with the steps.

2. Reinforcement Activity

Role Play:

1. The teacher should ask for a volunteer and role-play using the "So?" strategy. The teacher can call the volunteer names such as those in the book: "You shoot like a girl" or "You hop with frogs in the lab." The student should be asked to respond with "So?" Discuss how each person felt playing their role.

2. Divide the class into pairs. Explain to the students they will take turns playing the role of Little Bill and Michael. When playing the role of Michael, their job is to say mean things to the other person. When playing the role of Little Bill, they should respond by saying "So?" How did the other student respond to just saying "So?"

3. After a few minutes of practicing, bring the class together as a whole group. Ask for a set of volunteers to role-play in front of the class. Discuss how the students performed in the role play. Discuss additional locations where students could try this strategy.

"SO?" Role Play

Directions: Team up with a partner. You and your partner are going to take turns playing the roles of Little Bill and Michael. When it is your turn to play the role of Michael, your job is to read several mean things to your partner. Whoever is playing the role of Little Bill should respond by saying "So?" At the end, discuss and write down how you felt when your partner answered by just saying "So?"

Michael (say these things during turn 1):

1. You dress funny.
2. Your eyes are on the back of your head.
3. You wear diapers.
4. Your desk is a mess.
5. You can't dance worth a hoot.
6. Your work is sloppy.
7. You look like an alien.
8. You have bed-head hair.
9. You did not do well on the test.
10. You have cooties.

Michael (say these things during turn 2):

1. Your shoes are too dirty.
2. You drink from a baby bottle.
3. You eat bugs.
4. Your pencil is too short.
5. You have bad breath.
6. You pick peppers in Pennsylvania.
7. You can't kick a ball.
8. You are in trouble with me.
9. Your pants are on backward.
10. You ride a tricycle.

Write down how you felt when your partner said, "So?"

Student 1: _____

Student 2: _____

Arthur's April Fool

Title: *Arthur's April Fool*
Author: Marc Brown
Illustrator: Marc Brown
Copyright: 1983
Publisher: Little, Brown
ISBN: 0-316-11196-1
Topic: Responding to bullying
Approximate Grade Levels: K–3

Book Summary:

Arthur and friends are preparing for the April Fool's assembly. Binky Barnes is bullying Arthur by taking his belongings and threatening to pulverize him. Arthur is nervous he will not be able to perform his April Fool's trick. During the show, Arthur thinks of a way to handle Binky Barnes and save his dignity.

Lesson Goal:

To teach students appropriate alternate methods for responding to bullies.

Prereading Activities:

Begin by asking students if they have ever watched the *Arthur* television show. When students respond yes, ask them to describe the Binky Barnes character. Students are likely to describe him as large, tough, and other characteristics of a bully (they may also use positive descriptors, too, such as funny and liking books). Describe a personal bullying incident. Conclude by saying that at one time or another, most of us have to deal with people who seem like bullies and that's the topic of this story.

During Reading:

Read the story aloud, pausing as needed to clarify information or story plot. Before Arthur solves the problem, stop and ask students to predict the solution using I SOLVE.

Postreading/Discussion Questions:

After reading the story, discuss it with students and ask questions such as the following:

1. What were Arthur and his friends preparing for?

2. Who is Binky Barnes? How did Arthur describe him?

3. What was Binky threatening to do to Arthur?

4. Has anyone ever threatened to beat you up? If so, how did you respond?

5. Who could you tell if you were having a problem like this?

6. How did Arthur feel when he saw Binky sitting in the front row of the auditorium?

7. What do you think Arthur was feeling when Binky volunteered to help him?

8. What was Arthur's great idea for tricking Binky?

9. Do you think Arthur thought of this idea before or during the show?

10. Why was Binky scared of Arthur's trick?

I SOLVE Strategy

Tell students they can't always rely on magic to help them solve problems but that problem solving requires careful thinking and help from others.

I: Identify the problem presented in the book.

➤ Arthur is threatened that Binky is going to beat him up.

S: Solutions to the problem?

    a. Book suggestion: Arthur thought of a magic trick, cutting Binky in half, which scared him so he stopped bothering Arthur.

    b. Arthur could have told his parents about the problem.

    c. He could have ignored him and walked away.

    d. Other:

O: Obstacles to the solutions?

    a. Book suggestion: It may be difficult to think of a magic trick that scares Binky.

    b. Parents may talk to the teacher, but it might not be soon enough.

    c. Ignoring him may not be effective.

    d. Other:

L: Look at the solutions again and choose one.

Discuss all possibilities and have students select an appropriate strategy.

V: Validate the solution by trying it.

E: Evaluate how the solution worked.

Did the solution work? If not, consider another solution from step **S**.

Extended Learning Activities

1. Problem-Solving Practice Scenario

> Picture yourself outside playing at the park. You are happily swinging when an older and much larger kid comes up to you and says, "Get off now, or else!" What would you do?

I: Identify the problem.

➤ A larger kid tells you to get off the swing.

S: Solutions to the problem?

    a.   Quickly get off the swing.

    b.   Say, "No, I was here first, but I'll be finished in two minutes."

    c.   Call for help from an adult.

    d.   Other:

O: Obstacles to the solutions?

    a.   He may leave you alone if you quickly get off the swing.

    b.   He may realize you won't give in to his bullying and wait the two minutes for you to finish. He may also push you off the swing.

    c.   An adult may not be close by to help.

    d.   Other:

L: Look at the solutions again and choose one.

Suggest that students may want to try letter **b** first, because this solution lets the bully know that when he threatens me, he will not get his way.

V: Validate the solution by trying it.

Tell students they would try the solution and see how the bully acted.

E: Evaluate how the solution worked.

If the bully waited the two minutes and then I got off, the problem is solved. If he still threatens you, return to step **S** and brainstorm new solutions as well as review the old solutions. Continue with the steps.

2. Reinforcement Activity

Begin by showing students a magic trick: ***The Disappearing Coin***.

Materials: One coin, a table to sit at, and a chair to sit in.

Begin by asking students what they would think if you could make a coin disappear. Display the coin in your hand, and then try to rub it into your elbow, announcing you are going to make it disappear! After a few moments, drop the coin onto the table and say it usually works better with the other hand.

Pick the coin up and pretend to put it into the other hand. Then, pretend to rub the coin into your elbow, while the hand that is really holding the coin goes up behind your ear. Drop the coin into the back of your shirt collar. Show that the coin has vanished, and both hands are absolutely empty!

Next, give students a piece of paper and ask them to fold it in half. On one side have them draw a picture of a time they have been called names, teased, or bullied. On the other side, have students draw a picture showing the "magical" way they solved, or want to solve, their problem. After students finish drawing, have them divide into groups of three or four and discuss their drawings. Conclude by remarking that we all usually feel hurt when teased, so it is important to remember how you would feel before teasing another person.

Magical Solutions

Directions: Fold this piece of paper in half. On one side draw a picture of a time when you were called names, teased, or bullied. On the other side, draw a picture of the "magical" solution for the problem. Write a sentence about each picture. Once you are finished, wait for the teacher's directions for discussing your picture.

PROBLEM _____   "MAGICAL" SOLUTION _____

The Ant Bully

Title: *The Ant Bully*
Author: John Nickle
Illustrator: John Nickle
Copyright: 1999
Publisher: Scholastic
ISBN: 0-590-39591-2
Topic: Responding to bullying
Approximate Grade Levels: K–3

Book Summary:

The neighborhood bully, Sid, always picks on Lucas, who wears funny glasses and a strange hat. In turn, Lucas bullies ants by squirting them with water—at least until the ants decide to shrink him to get back at him. Lucas begins to identify with the ants and realizes that they are hard workers. Through his adventures with the ants, he finds courage to help the ants as well as deal with Sid, the bully.

Lesson Goal:

To help students identify strategies for responding to bullies.

Prereading Activities:

Ask students if they have ever bullied anyone or anything such as insects. If students do not respond about bullying ants, probe and ask if they have ever intentionally stepped on an anthill. Most likely, many students have stepped on or intentionally destroyed an anthill. Ask them if they ever thought about how the ants felt. Did they consider themselves bullies? Show students the cover of the book and ask them to predict what happens to the boy on the cover when he bullies the ants.

During Reading:

Read the story aloud, discussing the pictures. Use the I SOLVE strategy when appropriate.

Postreading/Discussion Questions:

After reading the story, go through it again with students and ask questions such as the following:

1. Why do you think Sid, the bully, was mean to Lucas?

2. Should people bully others because they look different? Explain.

3. Why did Lucas begin to bully the ants?

4. How do you think Lucas felt when the queen said to him, "Don't you realize how long and hard we work to build what you destroy in seconds?"

5. What does the queen mean when she says, "Put him on trial"?

6. What did Lucas realize when helping the colony with their jobs?

7. Why was there an "awkward silence" when Lucas was talking with Rene and Speedy?

8. How did Lucas feel when he jumped on his father's face, and why did he do this?

9. How was Lucas able to gain courage?

10. How is Lucas able to solve the problem?

I SOLVE Strategy

Tell students that it is not always easy to solve problems with bullies, but with help from others, a solution can be found.

I: Identify the problem presented in the book.

> ➤ Sid, the bully, steals Lucas's hat and squirts water on him.

S: Solutions to the problem?

    a. Book solution: Sid, the bully, identifies with the ants and realizes that bullying the small ants is not courageous or brave.

    b. Ignore Sid.

    c. Tell an adult about the problem.

    d. Other:

O: Obstacles to the solutions?

    a. Book solution: Sid may not identify with the ants and then would still bully Lucas.

    b. If Lucas ignores Sid he may stop bullying him, or it might make Sid increase his bullying.

    c. By telling an adult, Lucas can make sure others know about the bullying problem and can talk with Sid or his parents about stopping.

    d. Other:

L: Look at the solutions again and choose one.

Which one could help you in the long run?

V: Validate the solution by trying it.

Try the solution you selected.

E: Evaluate how the solution worked.

Did the solution work? If not, consider another solution from step **S**.

Extended Learning Activities

1. Problem-Solving Practice Scenario

Imagine yourself on a summer day having a picnic on the lawn. You are enjoying your food when an old stray dog comes over to your picnic and watches you eat. "Get out of here, dog!" you say. "Get going, you old mutt, before I make you go." Pretend the dog answers you and says, "I am old and hungry. Why are you being such a mean bully?" What would you do?

I: Identify the problem.

> ➤ The dog thinks you are being a mean bully.

S: Solutions to the problem?

    a. Think about how the dog feels. Apologize to the dog and offer it some food or water.

    b. Locate an adult to help.

    c. Ignore the dog.

    d. Get a stick and threaten the dog.

    e. Other:

O: Obstacles to the solutions?

    a. The dog may eat or drink too much.

    b. An adult may not be close.

    c. The dog may decide to go away on his own.

    d. You would be acting like a bully.

    e. Other:

L: Look at the solutions again and choose one.

Suggest that students may want to try letter **a** first because this solution allows the dog to rest, and then try solution **b** also to find an adult for additional help. By using these two solutions, you are not acting like a bully.

V: Validate the solution by trying it.

Tell students they would try the solution and see how the dog responded.

E: Evaluate how the solution worked.

If the dog left after eating and drinking, the problem is solved. If he still remains, return to step **S** and brainstorm new solutions as well as review the old solutions. Continue with the steps.

2. Reinforcement Activity

Divide students into groups of three or four. Give each group a copy of "Boo-Hoo Bully" to play along with the playing cards. Tell students that Sid is sorry he was mean to Lucas and wants the ants to make him his original size. For this to happen, he has to say nice things to Lucas. The only problem is that sometimes he forgets. When this happens, the ants won't restore his size. Students are to help Sid by placing their marker at the end of the row and drawing a card. Read the words on the card. If it is a nice saying, they get to move forward. If they draw a saying that is not nice, they do not move forward and go back to the start. The first student to reach the center is the winner and brings Sid back to his normal size.

Name:_____ Date: _____

Boo-Hoo Bully

Directions for playing: Sid is sorry he was mean to Lucas and wants the ants to make him his original size. In order for this to happen, he has to say nice things to Lucas. The only problem is that sometimes he forgets. When this happens, the ants won't restore his size. Place your marker at the end of the row. Draw a card and read the saying. If it is a nice saying, you move forward. If you draw a saying that is not nice, you go back to the start. The first student to reach the center is the winner and brings Sid back to his normal size. Game board is on page 25.

Boo-Hoo Bully Word Cards

I like your smile.	You are strange.
You are sweet.	I don't like you.
Thank you for sharing.	Give me your pencil!
You're the best!	Go away!
Let's go play.	You wear ugly shoes.
Thanks for the help.	Way to go!
You are a good friend.	Give me your hat!
I like you.	Come play at my house.
You dress nice.	Would you like some candy?
I think you are cool.	Get out!

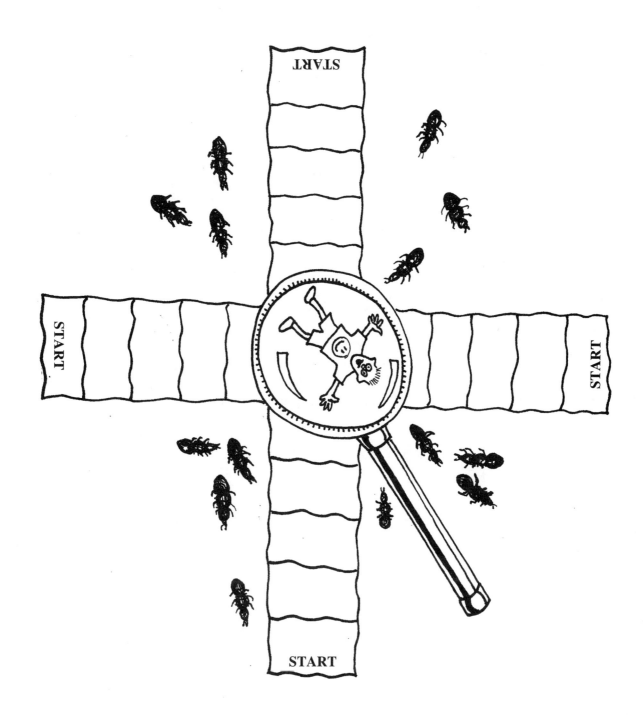

Louise Takes Charge

Title: *Louise Takes Charge*
Author: Stephen Krensky
Illustrator: Susanna Natti
Copyright: 1998
Publisher: Dial Books for Young Readers
ISBN: 0-8037-2306-7
Topic: Responding to bullying
Approximate Grade Levels: 1–3 (This is a chapter book.)

Book Summary:

When the new school year begins, Louise is confronted by Jasper, the class bully. Jasper picks on everyone in the class by taking food, bossing people around, and making them do his homework. Louise finally gets fed up with Jasper and holds a secret meeting to outsmart Jasper. By working together, Louise and her classmates turn the tables on Jasper and outwit their opponent.

Lesson Goal:

To help students realize that by working together, they can successfully confront a class bully.

Prereading Activities:

Begin by asking students to define or describe the term *bully*. Create a T chart with the students to list the characteristics of a bully.

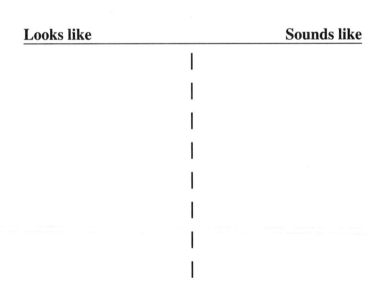

Bully

Looks like	Sounds like

Ask students if they have ever encountered a bully or a student with these characteristics (without using any individual student names). Discuss some of the possible reasons why children act like bullies. Allow students to share their stories. Once finished, display the book's cover and have students make predictions about the story.

During Reading:

Read aloud a chapter at a time. At the end of each chapter, discuss the following questions and ask students to predict what happens next. Use the I SOLVE strategy to predict how Louise solves the problem before reading about it in the book.

Postreading/Discussion Questions:

Chapter 1—How was Louise feeling when Jasper made the fist at her?

Chapter 2—What could the kids have done to get Jasper to pitch the ball better?

Chapter 3—Why does Jasper like to take things from other people's lunches?

Chapter 4—Why didn't Louise explain the problem to her father?

Chapter 5—What do you think the details are to Louise's plan?

Chapter 6—How is being Jasper's apprentice going to help Louise?

Chapter 7—What does Louise mean when she says, "Don't overdo your parts, guys"?

Chapter 8—Why did Jasper agree to allow Megan as an apprentice?

Chapter 9—Do you think the teacher would notice the unusual way Jasper was being treated by the classmates? Would he intervene?

Chapter 10—How is Jasper going to "unwant" his apprentices?

Chapter 11—How do you think Jasper felt when he realized that the classmates were not going to take his bullying anymore?

Chapter 12—How were Louise and her classmates feeling? Point out to students that Louise's plan took a long time to follow through, but that it was successful.

When people work together, they can overcome great problems.

I SOLVE Strategy

I: Identify the problem presented in the book.

> ➤ Jasper is being a bully by taking food, bossing people around, and making students complete his assignments.

S: Solutions to the problem?

    a.   Book solution: Louise realizes that they cannot conquer Jasper individually, so she meets with her classmates to devise a group plan to deal with him.

    b.   She could have discussed the problem with her parents.

    c.   Louise could have simply refused to give in to Jasper's demands.

    d.   Other:

O: Obstacles to the solutions?

    a.   Book solution: If students did not all work as a team, the plan would not have been successful.

    b.   Her parents could have helped Louise develop a plan, or they could have met with her teacher or school principal.

    c.   Jasper might hurt Louise if she refuses to give in to his demands.

    d.   Other:

L: Look at the solutions again and choose one.

Which one could help you in the long run?

V: Validate the solution by trying it.

Try the solution you selected.

E: Evaluate how the solution worked.

Did the solution work? If not, try your next solution.

Extended Learning Activities

1. Problem-Solving Practice Scenario

> Imagine that you have an older sister. At home she is very bossy, and when it is time for chores, she makes you do her chores, too. When you told her you were going to tell Mom about this, she threatened to sneak into your room at night and get you. What should you do?

I: Identify the problem.

   ➤ Your mean older sister is making you do her chores.

S: Solutions to the problem?

    a.   Tell your sister that you will keep doing her chores.

    b.   Tell your mom about the problem because you know Mom will not let her hurt you.

    c.   Tell your sister that she is not your boss and that you will not do her chores. Sleep with your door locked.

    d.   Other:

O: Obstacles to the solutions?

    a.   It is not fair if you keep doing her chores.

    b.   Your sister may find sneakier ways to get you.

    c.   Your sister may listen to you if you tell her in a nice way, but sleeping with the door locked would be difficult.

    d.   Other:

L: Look at the solutions again and choose one.

Suggest that students may want to try letter **b** first because in a situation where someone threatens you physically, it is always best to tell an adult as soon as possible.

V: Validate the solution by trying it.

Tell students they would try the solution and see how the sister reacted.

E: Evaluate how the solution worked.

If Mom talked with the sister and you and helped to improve the situation, the problem is solved. If she still remains bossy, tell your mom again and have a family meeting to brainstorm new solutions.

2. Reinforcement Activity

Divide students into groups. Tell students they are invited to Jasper's party but that Jasper wants their ideas for making the party a hit. Tell students they will need to work together to plan the menu, games, and their costume for the Egyptian party. Give them a copy of "Faster Jasper" to complete. Emphasize that by working together, they can make Jasper's party a success.

Name:_____   Date: _____

Faster Jasper

Directions: Now that Jasper is no longer acting like a bully, he wants to invite you to his party. He doesn't have much time before the party day so Jasper is asking for your help to make the party fun. In groups, discuss the menu and types of food you would like at the party, write about games to play, and draw a picture of costumes. By working together, your group can help make Jasper's party the best!

Name and describe the types of foods you would include at the party:

Describe, using details, games to play at Jasper's party:

Draw a picture of your costume here (or on the back):

Owen Foote, Frontiersman

Title: *Owen Foote, Frontiersman*
Author: Stephanie Greene
Illustrator: Martha Weston
Copyright: 1999
Publisher: Clarion Books
ISBN: 0-395-61578-X
Topic: Responding to bullying
Approximate Grade Levels: 2–3 (This is a chapter book.)

Book Summary:

Owen Foote, whose hero is Daniel Boone, built a tree fort in his neighbor's woods. He and his friend Joseph love spending time there. One day when they arrive at the fort, two older boys are in the fort making a mess and threatening to wreck the whole thing. Owen and Joseph must figure out a way to teach the bullies a lesson and save the tree fort.

Lesson Goal:

To teach students how to appropriately deal with bullies by developing a problem-solving plan.

Prereading Activities:

Ask students if they know the meaning of the word *frontiersman*. Tell them a frontiersman was a pioneer who lived long ago and explored America, such as Daniel Boone. Draw a Venn diagram on the board to highlight the unique differences as well as common similarities of a youngster who lived as a frontiersman with a youngster from today's era.

Explain to students that you will begin reading a story about Owen Foote, a youngster who likes to go into the woods and imagine that he is a frontiersman. Show students the cover of the book and ask them to make predictions. After the students' predictions, tell them the story is about how Owen deals with two bullies he meets in the woods.

During Reading:

Read aloud a chapter at a time. At the end of each chapter, discuss the guided questions and ask students to make predictions using the I SOLVE strategy when appropriate.

Postreading/Discussion Questions:

Chapter 1—Why didn't Owen tell Mrs. Greene about his tree fort?

Chapter 2—How did Owen and Joseph feel when they saw the boys in their fort? What do you think they felt like doing when they saw the boys?

Chapter 3—Why did Owen and Joseph give themselves animal names?

Chapter 4—What consequences do you think Owen's mother will give for walking out while she was talking?

Chapter 5—Why do you think Owen's mom allowed him to carry out his plan?

Chapter 6—Owen and Joseph's plan worked, but what would have happened if it hadn't?

Chapter 7—Why was Owen so confident when he saw the boys this time?

Chapter 8—Would you feel safe sleeping in the tree house? Why or why not?

I SOLVE Strategy

I: Identify the problem presented in the book.

➤ Two bullies threaten to wreck Owen's tree fort.

S: Solutions to the problem?
  a. Book solution: The boys developed a plan to scare the bullies away from their tree fort without hurting them.
  b. The boys could have told Mrs. Greene what happened in the woods.
  c. Other:

O: Obstacles to the solutions?
  a. Book solution: If the bullies were not scared of the boy's tricks, they would have wrecked the tree fort.
  b. Mrs. Greene could have been upset at Owen for building the tree fort.
  c. Other:

L: Look at the solutions again and choose one.
  Which one could help you in the long run? Perhaps telling Mrs. Greene would have quickly solved the problem.

V: Validate the solution by trying it.
  Try the solution you selected.

E: Evaluate how the solution worked.
  Did it work?

Extended Learning Activities

1. Problem-Solving Practice Scenario

Imagine you are riding your bicycle in your neighborhood when an older kid begins to call you mean names. What would you do?

I: Identify the problem.

> ➤ An older kid is calling you names.

S: Solutions to the problem?

     a. Call the kid mean names, too.

     b. Stop your bike and ask the kid to repeat what he said.

     c. Ignore the kid and keep riding away.

     d. Other:

O: Obstacles to the solutions?

     a. The mean kid might chase after you.

     b. Stopping your bike may make the kid call you even more names.

     c. Other:

L: Look at the solutions again and choose one.

Suggest that students may want to try letter **c** first because avoiding a conflict whenever possible is a smart idea. Telling an adult would help, too, because they can help solve the problem for the long run.

V: Validate the solution by trying it.

Tell students they would try the solution and see how it worked.

E: Evaluate how the solution worked.

If you got away from the mean kid and told an adult, the problem is solved. If he still calls you names, return to step **S** and brainstorm new solutions as well as review the old solutions. Continue with the steps.

2. Reinforcement Activity

Tell students they have a choice. They can write a letter either to Owen and Joseph or to a bully they know. If they write to Owen and Joseph, students can ask the boys specific questions about their adventures in the woods. Students should also tell Owen and Joseph how they would have handled the problem if they had been in the same situation. Allow students in the class to role-play being the bully and verbally respond to the letters. Give each student a copy of "Frontier Fan Mail" to complete. Students can illustrate their story on a separate piece of paper.

Name:_____ Date: _____

Frontier Fan Mail

Directions: Use this format to write a letter to Owen and Joseph. In your letter you can ask them any questions about their adventures in the woods. For example, you could ask them what they would do if the bullies returned. Also, tell Owen and Joseph how you would have handled the problem if you were in the same situation.

Additional Readings on Bullies

Title and Author: *The Two Bullies* by Junko Morimoto
ISBN: 0-517-80062-4
Approximate Grade Levels: K–3
Copyright: 1997

Book Summary:

Ni-ou is the strongest man in Japan. He hears about another man in China who is just as strong, so he travels to China to fight him and prove he is the strongest. Ni-ou finds quite a surprise when he arrives in China.

Title and Author: *Monster Boy* by Christine M. Winn
ISBN: 0-925-19087-X
Approximate Grade Levels: K–3
Copyright: 1996

Book Summary:

This story is about a bully who is transformed into a monster when he lets his temper rule his behavior. He decides to tame the monster and change back into a boy.

Title and Author: *Goggles* by Ezra Jack Keats
ISBN: 0-140-56440-3
Approximate Grade Levels: K–3
Copyright: 1998

Book Summary:

When Peter and his friend Archie find motorcycle goggles, some bigger boys try to take them away.

Helping Students Make and Keep Friends

It is important in life to have friends. The lesson plans in this chapter help teach students how to make, maintain, and maximize friendships. Students will also learn how to solve problems involving friends.

How to Be a Friend: A Guide to Making Friends and Keeping Them

Title: *How to Be a Friend: A Guide to Making Friends and Keeping Them*
Author: Laurie Krasny Brown
Illustrator: Marc Brown
Copyright: 1998
Publisher: Little, Brown
ISBN: 0-316-10913-4
Topic: Making and keeping friends
Approximate Grade Levels: K–3

Book Summary:

This book is part of the Dino Life Guides for Families series and examines all aspects of friendship including topics such as deciding who can be your friend, ways to be and not to be a friend, and talking out an argument. All pages are designed in cartoon format that allows for easy reading and discussion.

Lesson Goal:

To help children identify and discuss the complexities of making and keeping friends as well as successful strategies for interacting with friends.

Prereading Activities:

Begin by asking students what makes their friend a good friend. After listening to students, summarize by telling them that making and keeping friends can be a lot of work. Let them know that you are going to read a book about making friends. Tell them to listen to see if some of their suggestions on making friends are in the story.

During Reading:

This book is clearly divided with section headings. Read a section aloud. Before the book's solutions are revealed, stop reading and use the I SOLVE strategy to predict additional solutions.

Postreading/Discussion Questions:

1. What types of activities do you like to play by yourself?
2. What types of activities are best to play with a friend?
3. How do you show a friend that you like them?
4. If you feel left out, what can you do so that you won't hurt as much?
5. How can you overcome being shy?
6. When have you upset a friend and how did you make up?
7. What should you do if someone bullies you?
8. What do you think is the best way to make up with a friend?
9. Why is it important to solve an argument with a friend?
10. Why is it important to be friendly to other people?

I SOLVE Strategy

Explain to students that making and keeping friends requires some work. It is not always easy to make friends, but the more you practice, the easier it becomes.

I: Identify the problem presented in the book.

➤ One problem is that students do not know how to tell someone that they want to be their friend.

S: Solutions to the problem?

Book solutions for ways to be a friend include:

a. Protecting a friend if someone bothers him.
b. Sharing toys with friends.
c. Inviting friends to play with you.
d. Other:

O: Obstacles to the solutions?

Obstacles will vary according to individual children and their situations. You can discuss some obstacles such as there may not be many instances when they need to cheer up someone.

L: Look at the solutions again and choose one.

Which one could help you in the long run?

V: Validate the solution by trying it.

Try the solution that would help solve this problem.

E: Evaluate how the solution worked.

Extended Learning Activities

1. Problem-Solving Practice Scenario

Picture yourself eating lunch during school. One of your good friends asks you for your dessert and you say no. Your friend then says, "I don't like you anymore." What would you do?

I: Identify the problem.

> Your friend said something that hurt your feelings.

S: Solutions to the problem?

a. Decide to share a small piece of dessert with your friend.

b. Tell your friend that you still like them, even though you won't share your dessert.

c. Ignore your friend because you know they are just upset and will get over it.

d. Other:

O: Obstacles to the solutions?

a. You will have less dessert to eat.

b. Your friend may still be upset with you.

c. Your friend may say more things that hurt your feelings.

d. Other:

L: Look at the solutions again and choose one.

Help students understand it is all right if someone does not want to share their dessert. However, if the person is a good friend, then they probably would share their dessert.

V: Validate the solution by trying it.

Tell students to try the solution and see how their friend reacted.

E: Evaluate how the solution worked.

If the friend understood that this was a very special dessert, then the problem would be solved. If your friend still did not understand or continued to be upset, return to step **S** and see if any other solutions might work. Continue with the steps.

2. Reinforcement Activity

Give each student a copy of the activity on ways to be a friend. Tell students to draw a picture in each section of the paper (four sections in all) showing things they do with friends. Ask students to write a sentence or two describing each picture. Share pictures if time permits.

Name:_____ Date: _____

Ways to Be a Friend

Directions: In each section draw a picture showing something you did to be a friend. Write about each picture.

The All-New Amelia

Title: *The All-New Amelia*
Author: Marissa Moss
Illustrator: Marissa Moss
Copyright: 1999
Publisher: First Pleasant Company
ISBN: 1-56247-840-0
Topic: Keeping friends
Approximate Grade Level: 3

Book Summary:

Amelia is impressed by the beauty and elegance of a new girl in her class. She tries to change herself to be more like the new girl but almost loses her true friend in the process.

Lesson Goal:

To help students realize that being a loyal friend is more important than trying to impress a new person.

Prereading Activities:

Brainstorm a list of characteristics describing a best friend. Ask students if they have ever argued with their best friend and share examples of arguments and how they were resolved. Show students the cover of the book and ask them to predict the story plot based on the title.

During Reading:

Read the story aloud. You may want to read one section at a time to students or the entire story if time permits. This book is structured so that the teacher can stop and allow the class to predict how Amelia solves her problem and then apply the I SOLVE strategy.

Postreading/Discussion Questions:

After reading the entire story or each section, examine it again with students and ask questions such as the following:

1. What made Amelia start thinking about the way her face looks?

2. Why does Charisse appear so attractive to Amelia?

3. Do you think Amelia was boring to Charisse?

4. Have you ever liked what someone else was doing so you started acting that way, too?

5. Do you agree with Amelia that using an accent is self-improvement?

6. Have you ever looked in the mirror and felt like the face you saw was not your own?

7. Amelia says, "I feel like I'm bad at EVERYTHING now!" Explain what she means and how you think she should handle the situation.

8. Amelia's best friend, Carly, blew up at her because of the phony way she was acting. Why?

9. How did Amelia finally realize that she was trying to improve herself for the wrong reasons?

10. How hard to you think it was for Amelia to apologize to Carly?

I SOLVE Strategy

Tell students that it is not always easy to solve problems with friends but that by solving the problem, it helps the friendship grow stronger.

I: Identify the problem presented in the book.

➤ Amelia's best friend feels neglected and becomes angry.

S: Solutions to the problem?

a. Book solution: Amelia realizes, through self-reflection and the actions of others around her, that trying to improve herself by acting phony is causing others to like her less.

b. Amelia could have continued to act like the "new" Amelia.

c. Amelia could have approached Charisse and talked about similarities and differences between British and American kids.

d. Other:

O: Obstacles to the solutions?

a. Book solution: Amelia finally realized that maintaining a relationship with her best friend was more important than trying to establish a relationship with the new student. There are no major obstacles to this solution.

b. If Amelia continued to act like the new Amelia, she would have continued to distance herself from her best friend, and it was likely that Charisse still would not have paid much attention to her.

c. If Amelia approached Charisse to talk, she may have talked with her or rejected Ameila's efforts. If she rejected Amelia's repeated efforts, then it is an indication that Charisse is not going to be a good friend.

d. Other:

L: Look at the solutions again and choose one.

Which one could help you in the long run?

V: Validate the solution by trying it.

Try the solution you selected.

E: Evaluate how the solution worked.

Did the solution work? If not, try your next solution.

Extended Learning Activities

1. Problem-Solving Practice Scenario

> Picture a beautiful day outside. You are playing in front of your house. Your best friend lives across the street, and the front door of the house begins to open. Excited, you run to see who is coming out of the house and see it's your best friend with another kid you do not know. You feel so disappointed. What would you do?

I: Identify the problem.

> ➤ Your best friend has another friend over and you don't know who it is.

S: Solutions to the problem?

    a.   Walk over to your friend's house and ask him or her to play.

    b.   Wait to see if your friend notices you and says, "Hi."

    c.   Other:

O: Obstacles to the solutions?

    a.   Your friend may introduce you to the stranger and invite you to play.

    b.   Your friend may not invite you to play or even say, "Hi."

    c.   Other:

L: Look at the solutions again and choose one.

Since this is your best friend, you should think about going to their house to find out what's happening.

V: Validate the solution by trying it.

Choose the solution you will feel comfortable with.

E: Evaluate how the solution worked.

If your solution was successful, try it again next time a similar situation occurs.

2. Reinforcement Activity

Begin by dividing the class into pairs. Instruct students to take turns role-playing the characters of Amelia and Carly. When a student role-plays the "all-new" Amelia, he or she should try to act and talk just like her, based on the book description. When playing Carly's role, the student should question Amelia about her phony acting.

After completing the role play for approximately 10 minutes, ask students to make a journal entry explaining their experience. Ask students to write about a personal experience involving an argument with their best friend.

Name:_____ Date:_____

Journal Experience

Directions: Take turns role-playing the characters of Amelia and Carly. When you role-play the "all-new" Amelia, try to act and talk like her based on the book description. When playing Carly's role, question Amelia about her phony acting. After a few minutes, the teacher will announce to switch roles. After completing the role play, make a journal entry explaining your experience. Write about a personal experience involving an argument with a friend. Tell how the argument started and how it was resolved.

_____

_____

_____

_____

_____

_____

_____

_____

_____

_____

_____

Super-Fine Valentine

Title: *Super-Fine Valentine*
Author: Bill Cosby
Illustrator: Varnette P. Honeywood
Copyright: 1998
Publisher: Scholastic
ISBN: 0-590-95622-1 (paperback); 0-590-16401-5 (hardcover)
Topic: Peer pressure from friends
Approximate Grade Levels: K–3

Book Summary:

Little Bill likes Mia and makes her a special valentine. He has difficulty giving her the valentine because the other kids are teasing him.

Lesson Goal:

To help students realize that it is important to express your feelings for someone even if others tease. Children need to know that liking someone special is a natural feeling.

Prereading Activities:

Show students the cover of the book and ask them to make predictions about the story. Discuss the meaning of Valentine's Day with students. Ask students if they have ever given someone special a card to express their feelings. Read the book aloud and find out if students' predictions were accurate.

During Reading:

Read the story aloud, stopping at the end of each chapter to have students make predictions. Stop reading before the solution is read and permit students to predict the outcome.

Postreading/Discussion Questions:

1. What was Little Bill's secret?

2. What happened to Little Bill that was bad?

3. How did Little Bill feel when Andrew said, "Little Bill is in love with Mia!"?

4. Why was Little Bill looking for Mia after school?

5. Why did Little Bill run when Julia called him? How was he feeling?

6. Why did Little Bill get dressed and eat breakfast without being told?

7. Has your heart ever been scared to do something? Explain.

8. Why would Little Bill throw his card for Mia in the recycling bin?

9. What did Little Bill's friends do that helped him?

10. How do you think Mia felt when Little Bill gave her the valentine?

I SOLVE Strategy

Tell students that it is not always easy to tell someone you like them, especially when you worry about others teasing. Let them know it is okay and natural to show people you like them.

I: Identify the problem presented in the book.

> ➤ Little Bill is worried that the kids in his class will tease him if he gives Mia a valentine.

S: Solutions to the problem?

  a. Book solution: First, Little Bill throws the valentine he made away. Once he realizes others gave Mia valentines, he gives her one, too.

  b. Little Bill could have given Mia the valentine right after she gave him one.

  c. Little Bill could have told his friends to stop teasing.

  d. Other:

O: Obstacles to the solutions?

  a. Book solution: By throwing the valentine in the recycling bin, Little Bill would miss an opportunity to tell Mia he likes her.

  b. If Little Bill gave Mia the valentine right away, his friends may have teased him.

  c. It may be difficult for Little Bill to stand up to his friends and tell them to stop, but they might listen.

  d. Other:

L: Look at the solutions again and choose one.

  Which one could help you in the long run?

V: Validate the solution by trying it.

  Try the solution you selected. Suggest students may want to try **b**, since this is a natural time to exchange valentines.

E: Evaluate how the solution worked.

  Did the solution work? If not, try the next solution with fewer obstacles.

Extended Learning Activities

1. Problem-Solving Practice Scenario

> Picture that you got a new haircut and one of your friends starts to tease you about the way it looks. What would you do? How would you act?

I: Identify the problem.

> ➤ A friend is teasing you about your new haircut.

S: Solutions to the problem?

    a. Tell the friend that teasing is hurting your feelings and you want them to stop.

    b. Tease your friend about their hair.

    c. Other:

O: Obstacles to the solutions?

    a. Your friend may see that the teasing bothers you and may decide not to stop.

    b. Your friend may laugh when you begin to tease.

    c. Other:

L: Look at the solutions again and choose one.

Choose a peaceful solution that would help to prevent the problem from happening again.

V: Validate the solution by trying it.

Tell students they would try the solution, such as **a**, that would peacefully solve the problem.

E: Evaluate how the solution worked.

If the solution did not solve the problem, return to the **S** step and review other possibilities.

2. Reinforcement Activity

Give students the reinforcement activity sheet, "Pleasant Poem," and explain that they will write a poem for a person they care about. On the first line, they write the person's name. The second line should contain two words describing how they feel about the person. The third line should contain two things the person does well. The fourth line should be a word about your feelings. You may want students to draw a picture of the person they care about.

Pleasant Poem

Directions: Follow the instructions from your teacher to complete the poem using the form on the next page. You may use some of the words from the box in your poem. Below is an example.

love	appreciate	special	wonderful	kind	patient
generous	thoughtful	happy	funny	caring	giving
nice	lovable	helpful	warm	sweet	good

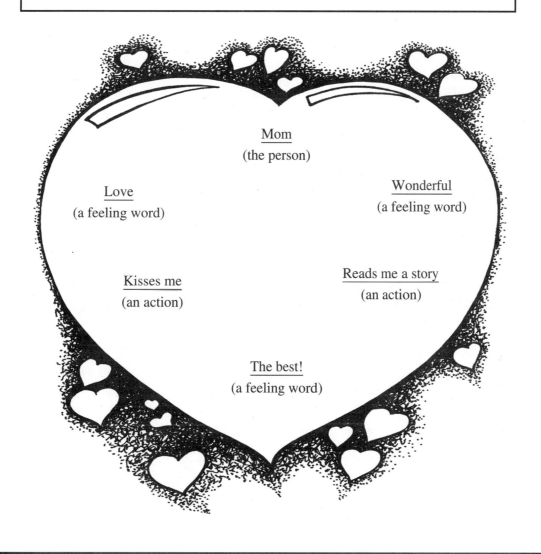

Mom
(the person)

Love
(a feeling word)

Wonderful
(a feeling word)

Kisses me
(an action)

Reads me a story
(an action)

The best!
(a feeling word)

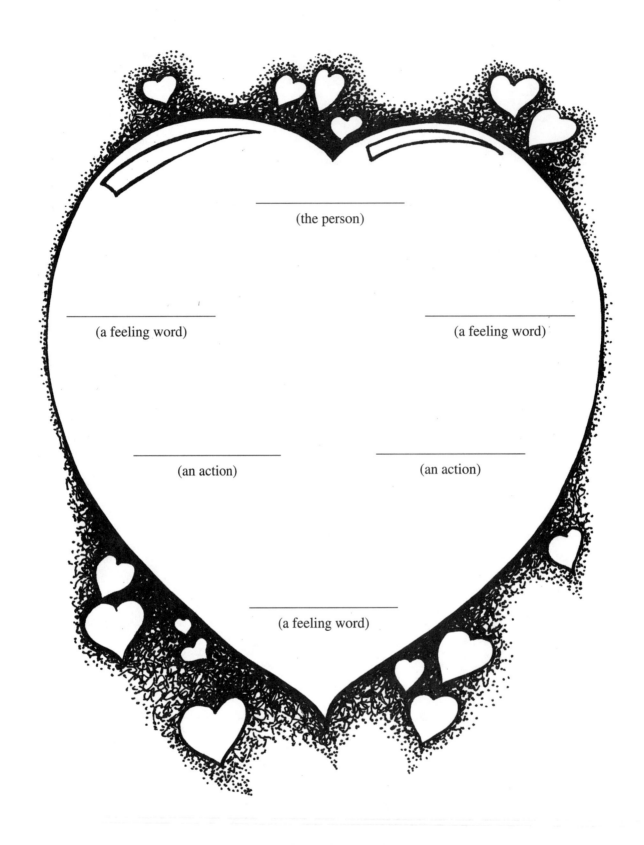

_____
(the person)

_____
(a feeling word)

_____
(a feeling word)

_____
(an action)

_____
(an action)

_____
(a feeling word)

Arthur and the Popularity Test

Title: *Arthur and the Popularity Test*
Author: Marc Brown
Illustrator: Marc Brown
Copyright: 1998
Publisher: Little, Brown
ISBN: 0-316-11545-2 (paperback); 0-316-11544-4 (hardcover)
Topic: Popularity and self-concept
Approximate Grade Level: 3 (This is a chapter book.)

Book Summary:

Arthur and his friends find a popularity test in a teenage magazine. When Sue Ellen and Fern take the test, they find out that Sue Ellen needs to tone things down, and Fern needs to become more assertive. The rest of the gang does not like the changes and wonders what's going on.

Lesson Goal:

To help children realize our friends accept us for ourselves and that changing to be like someone else will not increase our popularity.

Prereading Activities:

Begin by asking students to raise their hands if they have ever taken a test. Once students raise their hands, ask them if they have ever taken a popularity test. Tell students that Arthur and his friends take a popularity test in the book. Ask students to make predictions about the types of questions on a popularity test. Have students make predictions about the most popular student in the story.

During Reading:

Read the story aloud, stopping at the end of each chapter to have students make predictions.

Postreading/Discussion Questions:

Chapter 1—Why are the kids putting so many different things in their backpacks?

Chapter 2—How did Fern feel when the kids told her the poem was not a good idea?

Chapter 3—What would you learn from these types of popularity questions?

Chapter 4—Why would Fern and Sue Ellen want to take the popularity test after everyone left?

Chapter 5—Do you think the girls reacted the right way once they determined the meaning of their scores?

Chapter 6—Why were all the kids staring at Sue Ellen and Fern?

Chapter 7—Do you think the girls' plan is working out the way they anticipated?

Chapter 8—Did the girls make a mistake? Why?

Chapter 9—How do you think the girls felt when Arthur said, "We like you the way you are"?

Chapter 10—Why was Binky happy to have a rematch with Sue Ellen?

I SOLVE Strategy

Would you take a test to find out how much other people like you? If you are in a similar situation, try these problem-solving steps instead.

I: Identify the problem presented in the book.

> ➤ Fern and Sue Ellen find out from the "popularity test" that people want them to act differently.

S: Solutions to the problem?

  a. Book solution: The girls changed their actions and found out that their friends liked them just the way they were.

  b. The girls could have left the magazine in the garbage.

  c. The girls could have showed the test to an adult.

  d. Other:

O: Obstacles to the solutions?

  a. Book solution: Things seemed to go a little wild in chapter 8 before the girls began to realize they made a mistake.

  b. If the girls left the magazine in the garbage, the problem would have never started.

  c. If the girls showed the test to an adult, they may have been embarrassed or thought they would get in trouble.

  d. Other:

L: Look at the solutions again and choose one.

  Which one could help you in the long run?

V: Validate the solution by trying it.

  Try the solution you selected. If students try solution **b**, the problem would have been avoided.

E: Evaluate how the solution worked.

  Did it work? If not, look at the possible solutions again.

Extended Learning Activities

1. Problem-Solving Practice Scenario

Imagine that one of your friends in the class is having a birthday party and invites all the kids in the class except you. Can you solve this problem? How?

I: Identify the problem.

➤ You are the only person in the class not invited to a birthday party.

S: Solutions to the problem?

   a. Pretend that you do not care about going to the birthday party so the person does not see that they can make you upset.

   b. Talk to the person and ask them why they did not invite you.

   c. Other:

O: Obstacles to the solutions?

   a. The person may never mention going to the party again.

   b. Talking to the person may feel uncomfortable, but it lets the person know how you feel.

   c. Other:

L: Look at the solutions again and choose one.

Does one solution seem better than the others?

V: Validate the solution by trying it.

Try the solution that makes you feel good about yourself.

E: Evaluate how the solution worked.

Try another solution or ask an adult for help if the first solution did not work.

2. Reinforcement Activity

Give students a copy of the activity "Positive Powers" so they can develop a rap or song that highlights their strengths.

Next, give students this sample popularity quiz: If you were with your friends after school laughing and having a good time, what color would your friends use to describe you? (A) red, (B) yellow, (C) blue, (D) black. Ask students to write down their answer.

Provide students with the "answers." If they choose the color red, their friends think they are easily angered. Students who choose yellow are considered too mellow and shy, those who choose blue are calm and cool, and those who choose black are confident.

Ask students what they learned about themselves and others from this quiz. Reinforce their responses that this "quiz" did not teach them anything about themselves or have anything to do with popularity. Many times we overlook our strengths and do not give ourselves credit. Tell students to compose a rap, song, or poem that describes their strengths and will give others insight into their inner beauty.

Name:_____   Date: _____

Positive Powers

Directions: Write a song or rap that describes your strengths.

Example:

> Football, dance, piano, or swimming,
> in any sport I'm usually winning.
>
> My body is a machine and finely tuned,
> from working out in the weight room.
>
> I've got incredible feet,
> and I know I'll earn millions playing for the Miami Heat.

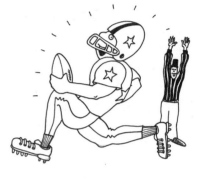

_____

_____

_____

_____

_____

_____

_____

_____

_____

_____

_____

_____

How Humans Make Friends

Title: *How Humans Make Friends*
Author: Loreen Leedy
Illustrator: Loreen Leedy
Copyright: 1996
Publisher: Holiday House
ISBN: 0-8234-1223-7
Topic: Making friends
Approximate Grade Levels: K–3

Book Summary:

This book is written from the viewpoint of an alien who came to Earth and found out how humans make friends. The alien explains how humans meet, the types of things we do together, feelings of friends, why friends don't get along, having and resolving conflicts, and types of friendships. The book is written using a question-and-answer cartoon format.

Lesson Goal:

To help students identify how people make and keep friends as well as resolve problems with friends.

Prereading Activities:

Give students a piece of paper and ask them to draw a friend. Allow them a few minutes to share their pictures with the class or with a partner. Once they are finished, comment that no one drew a picture of an alien friend. Show the class the cover of the book and tell them that in the book you are going to read, an alien gives a report on how humans make friends.

During Reading:

Read the story aloud, pausing as needed to clarify information. Ask the class to predict the book solution using the I SOLVE strategy.

Postreading/Discussion Questions:

After reading the story ask questions such as the following:

1. Can you think of any other places where you might meet friends?

2. What types of words do friends use when they meet each other?

3. What do you talk about with your friends?

4. What can you talk about when you meet a friend for the first time?

5. What are some of the things friends do for each other?

6. What are some things that cause friendships to get in trouble?

7. When our feelings are hurt, what types of things can help us feel better?

8. When have you and a friend experienced a conflict?

9. How can you show a friend that you are sorry about the argument?

10. Why are there different types of friendships?

I SOLVE Strategy

I: Identify the problem presented in the book.

➤ Sometimes friends have conflicts.

S: Solutions to the problem?

    a. Book suggestions: First, understand your feelings. You may be feeling shocked, hurt, tense, disappointed, sad, mad, or embarrassed.

    b. Next, realize that it's all right to admit mistakes, apologize, and forgive.

    c. Other:

O: Obstacles to the solutions?

    a. Book suggestions: Sometimes it is hard to recognize our own feelings. It is important to pause and think about how we feel before reacting to someone.

    b. Some people feel embarrassed to apologize or admit their mistakes. Apologizing takes practice and may feel awkward at first.

    c. Other:

L: Look at the solutions again and choose one.

Which one should students select? Discuss all possibilities and have students identify the best strategy to try first.

V: Validate the solution by trying it.

Students should have many opportunities to try the strategy you recommend.

E: Evaluate how the solution worked.

Was it successful? If not, return to step **S** to review the remaining solutions and choose the next solution with the least obstacles.

Extended Learning Activities

1. Problem-Solving Practice Scenario

> It's the middle of the school year, and a new student joins your class. During recess you see the new student sitting alone on a bench. How can you start a conversation? What should you do?

I: Identify the problem.

➤ You are not sure how to start talking with the new student.

S: Solutions to the problem?

    a.   Walk up to the student and ask him or her if they want to play.

    b.   Pretend you need to rest and then sit next to the new student on the bench. Begin talking.

    c.   Other:

O: Obstacles to the solutions?

    a.   The student may say either yes or no.

    b.   The student could be shy or just choose to ignore you even if you started talking.

    c.   Other:

L: Look at the solutions again and choose one.

Think of how you would feel if you were new in the class.

V: Validate the solution by trying it.

If the student does not talk much, try again another time.

E: Evaluate how the solution worked.

You could even decide to bring another person with you to meet the new student.

2. Reinforcement Activity

Give students a piece of construction paper, crayons, and copies of old magazines. Allow students to draw or cut out pictures to make a collage of people who look like friends. Students can also look for people who may be having an argument and tell about how they think the people can solve their argument peacefully. Allow students to write a sentence or two on the back of the collage describing their picture. Display the collages on a friendship bulletin board.

Name:_____ Date: _____

Friendship Collage

Directions: Use this piece of paper or construction paper to create a friendship collage. Cut pictures out of magazines or draw pictures showing things you like to do with your friends or pictures of people who look like friends. You can also look for pictures of friends having an argument. Write about how you think the friends can solve their problem.

Additional Readings on Friendship

Title and Author: *Making Friends* by Fred Rogers
ISBN: 0-808-58962-8
Approximate Grade Levels: K–2
Copyright: 1999

Book Summary:

The basics of friendship are covered and illustrated with photographs. The issues covered include friends becoming angry with one another, sharing things, waiting one's turn, how it feels if a friend does not want to play with you, and the positive benefits of friendship.

Title and Author: *Will I Have a Friend?* by Miriam Cohen
ISBN: 0-02-722790-1
Approximate Grade Levels: K–2
Copyright: 1967

Book Summary:

A young boy named Jim is just starting school. He wonders if he will have any friends at school. Jim tries to get involved with other kids. He passes out the cookies at snack time and talks to another boy, but his mouth is too full to talk. Finally, during rest time, Paul looks at him. He shows Jim his truck, and they begin to play together and with other kids, too. Jim is happy he made a friend.

Title and Author: *Horace and Morris but Mostly Dolores* by James Howe
ISBN: 0-689-31874-X
Approximate Grade Levels: K–3
Copyright: 1999

Book Summary:

Horace, Morris, and Dolores are best mice friends who love to do everything together. One day Horace and Morris decide they do not want anything to do with Dolores, and they build a boy's clubhouse. Dolores builds a girl's clubhouse. Many days later Dolores decides she is bored and wants to go exploring. She and a friend, Chloris, ask the boys to come along. Then Horace, Morris, Boris, Dolores, and Chloris decide it is best to build their own clubhouse that includes everyone.

Helping Students Avoid Fighting

Chapter 4

Many times students find themselves in situations where they feel like responding by fighting. The lesson plans in this chapter contain ideas for teaching students positive alternatives to fighting and reinforce students' physical safety.

Why Are You Fighting, Davy?

Title: *Why Are You Fighting, Davy?*
Author: Brigitte Weninger
Illustrator: Eve Tharlet
Copyright: 1999
Publisher: North-South Books
ISBN: 0-7358-1073-7 (paperback); 0-7358-1074-5 (hardcover)
Topic: Fighting
Approximate Grade Levels: K–2

Book Summary:
Davy and his best friend Eddie get into a fight while playing. Davy storms home and tells Mother he is never playing with Eddie again. After some cooldown time, the friends realize their strengths complement each other and they reconcile.

Lesson Goal:
To help children understand that arguing is natural but that it is important to peacefully reconcile.

Prereading Activities:

Begin by asking students the question "Why do people argue or fight with each other?" After listening to some of their examples, reinforce that it is all right to argue as long as we learn from the argument. Also, stress that it is important to solve arguments peacefully by talking about them rather than by using physical actions.

During Reading:

Read the story aloud, stopping periodically to have students make predictions and use the I SOLVE strategy.

Postreading/Discussion Questions:

1. What are the things that Davy and Eddie are good at building?

2. What happened that caused the friends to argue?

3. What could Davy have done instead of shouting at Eddie?

4. How did Eddie feel when he was shouted at? Have you felt this way before?

5. Why would Davy pull Eddie's ear? What caused them to stop fighting?

6. Why did Eddie say, "You're not my friend anymore. I never want to see you again"?

7. What did Davy play once he was home? How did he begin to feel?

8. What did Davy and Eddie learn when they tried to build something together?

9. How did the friends start to get along again? What happened?

10. Did Davy ever apologize for pulling on Eddie's ear?

I SOLVE Strategy

Students should realize that arguing with a friend happens to everyone, and sometimes the person who apologizes is the more confident person.

I: Identify the problem presented in the book.

➤ Davy gets mad and pulls Eddie's ear, so Eddie pulls Davy's ear.

S: Solutions to the problem?

a. Book solution: The boys go home and cool down from the argument. Later, they each start to play and realize they need each other's talents to make a boat and dam, so they begin playing together again.

b. Once they were cooled down, the boys could have apologized to each other.

c. The boys could have stayed angry at each other.

d. Other:

O: Obstacles to the solutions?

    a. Book solution: The boys solve the argument by being nice to each other and accepting of each other's suggestions.

    b. If the boys apologized to each other at their houses, this may have allowed them to play together more quickly.

    c. If the boys remained angry, they would not have played together again.

    d. Other:

L: Look at the solutions again and choose one.

    Which one could help you in the long run?

V: Validate the solution by trying it.

    Try the solution you selected. Suggest the students may want to try the book's solution.

E: Evaluate how the solution worked.

    How did the solution work? If the problem is not solved, return to step **S** and consider the remaining solutions.

Extended Learning Activities

1. Problem-Solving Practice Scenario

> Imagine that you are an excellent skateboarder. You want a ramp to practice skateboarding moves on, but you do not know how to build one. One of your friends is good at building things but is not a good skateboarder. How could you help each other and solve this problem?

I: Identify the problem.

    ➤ You want to build a skateboarding ramp but do not know how.

S: Solutions to the problem?

    a. Call your friend who knows how to build things and ask for help. Offer to teach your friend some moves if he or she helps you.

    b. Locate a book that shows how to build a ramp and try making it yourself.

    c. Other:

O: Obstacles to the solutions?

    a.   Your friend may say no.

    b.   It may be difficult to locate a book on ramp building.

    c.   Other:

L: Look at the solutions again and choose one.

Start with the solution that is beneficial for you and your friend.

V: Validate the solution by trying it.

Suggest that students try solution **a** if appropriate.

E: Evaluate how the solution worked.

If the solution worked, then you are happy! If not, try another solution.

2. Reinforcement Activity

Give each student a copy of "Rules for Fixing Fights." Divide students into pairs, or as a whole class activity ask students to think about a time when they had a fight or argument with a friend. Explain that if friends agree on rules for fighting ahead of time, they can help solve arguments more quickly. For example, students may agree to separate for two minutes and then sit down and talk out the problem. Ask students to discuss and then write several rules for fighting fair. Share everyone's rules as a class when finished.

Name:_____ Date: _____

Rules for Fixing Fights

Directions: Think about a recent argument you had with a friend. Discuss what happened and how you solved the argument. Write down several rules for fixing fights that could help you solve an argument. Draw a picture when finished.

Example Rules:

1. If needed, separate for a few minutes.
2. Tell the person how you feel.
3. Listen to the other person.
4. Decide on a solution everyone likes.

Our Rules for Fighting Fair

Created by: _____ and _____

1. _____

   _____

2. _____

   _____

3. _____

   _____

4. _____

   _____

5. _____

   _____

Dealing with Fighting

Title: *Dealing with Fighting*
Author: Marianne Johnston
Copyright: 1996
Publisher: Rosen Publishing Group
ISBN: 0-8239-2373-8
Topic: Fighting
Approximate Grade Levels: K–3

Book Summary:

> This book is organized into 10 sections that include topics such as how a fight starts, how to stop a fight before it starts, and how to talk instead of fight. Three scenarios with kids illustrate the main points in the book. This book discusses appropriate ideas for solving arguments and contains photographs.

Lesson Goal:

> To teach students how to peacefully resolve arguments.

Prereading Activities:

> Create a brainstorm with the students about fighting. Write the word *fighting* on the board and circle it. Ask students to tell you some ideas they have when they see the word *fighting*. As you write the words on the board, try to organize them into categories. After creating the brainstorm, have students notice if most of the comments are positive or negative. Summarize by telling students that most of the time, fighting does not resolve problems and makes everyone feel bad. Show them the book cover and begin reading the story.

During Reading:

> Read the book aloud and use the I SOLVE strategy to allow students to predict the book's solution before you read it aloud.

Postreading/Discussion Questions:

1. How do fights usually start?
2. What does verbal fighting mean?
3. Why are verbal fights unproductive?
4. What happens when people physically fight?
5. What would you do to solve the argument if you were Sean and Albert?
6. How does staying calm help you during an argument?
7. When you feel like fighting, what question should you ask yourself?
8. What do you think Keisha and Darren said to each other to solve their argument?
9. What is the best way to resolve a conflict? Why?
10. Why is it often hard to compromise?

I SOLVE Strategy

Students should realize that talking is the best way to resolve an argument. Fighting should always be avoided.

I: Identify the problem presented in the book.

➤ Verbal and physical fighting are the problems presented.

S: Solutions to the problem?

a. Book solution: One suggestion the book makes is to stay calm and listen. Each person should take turns talking and listening.

b. When you feel like fighting, walk away and calm down.

c. Talk out the problem and try to say exactly how you feel.

d. Compromise, if needed, to help solve the problem.

e. Other:

O: Obstacles to the solutions?

a. Book solution: The book provides concrete and meaningful solutions to fighting. One obstacle would be if one person refused to talk.

b. You may need to count to 10 to calm down.

c. Think for a few minutes about exactly how you feel before you begin talking.

d. Compromising is difficult, and you shouldn't always be the only one to compromise.

e. Other:

L: Look at the solutions again and choose one.

Which one could help you in the long run?

V: Validate the solution by trying it.

Try the solution you selected. Solution **a** suggests that students talk about their problems.

E: Evaluate how the solution worked.

If the solution did not solve the problem, return to step **S** and review the remaining solutions.

Extended Learning Activities

1. Problem-Solving Practice Scenario

Imagine that you are walking in line to lunch and do not notice the students in front of you are stopping. You bump right into the student in front of you. Without saying a word, he turns around and pushes you down on the ground. You are not hurt, but you are mad. What should you do?

I: Identify the problem.

➤ You bump into the student in front of you and he pushes you on the ground.

S: Solutions to the problem?

     a.   You could stand up and apologize for bumping into the student.

     b.   You could stand up and push the other student on the ground.

     c.   Other:

O: Obstacles to the solutions?

     a.   If you apologize, then the other student may apologize for pushing you down.

     b.   If you push the other student to the ground, it may start a physical fight.

     c.   Other:

L: Look at the solutions again and choose one.

Choose the solution that would resolve the problem without anyone getting hurt.

V: Validate the solution by trying it.

Try the solution, or call for the teacher's help if you feel threatened.

E: Evaluate how the solution worked.

Were you able to solve the situation peacefully? If not, what other solutions might work?

2. Reinforcement Activity

Give each student a copy of "Fighting Fair Role Play." Divide students into groups of three. In each group of three, students take turns role-playing the two arguing students and one referee who monitors to ensure students are following the rules for fighting fair. The role plays are related to the scenarios presented in the book. Students need to bring the rules for fixing fights, which they developed in the previous story, *Why Are You Fighting, Davy?*

Name:_____   Date: _____

Fighting Fair Role Play

Directions: In your groups, each person should take turns role-playing the arguer and the referee. Read the scenarios presented and role-play using the "rules for fixing fights" that you developed in a previous lesson. When you are finished, write the most important things you learned about solving arguments.

Scenario One:

Sean and Albert yelled at each other because they could not decide what video to watch. Sean punched Albert and both boys were not allowed to watch television for a week. Use your rules for fighting fair to solve this argument before it turns physical.

Scenario Two:

Keisha and Darren were arguing over what computer game to play. Keisha became so angry that she wanted to hit Darren when he called her names. Use your rules for fighting fair to solve this argument.

Scenario Three:

Tina and Chris were playing when Tina let Chris borrow her bike. Chris fell off the bike and accidentally broke one of the pedals. Tina called Chris a dummy, and Chris threw the bike on the ground. Use your rules for fighting fair to solve this argument.

Summary:

The most important things I learned about arguing are: _____

_____

Dealing with Arguments

Title: *Dealing with Arguments*
Author: Lisa K. Adams
Copyright: 1997
Publisher: Rosen Publishing Group
ISBN: 0-8239-5073-5
Topic: Arguing
Approximate Grade Levels: K–3

Book Summary:

This book defines and provides examples of arguments using photographs of children of different ages. Ten sections of the book discuss how arguments start, how to compromise, and how to avoid arguments.

Lesson Goal:

To help children understand that arguing is natural, but it is equally important to solve the argument using a calm voice and without physical fighting.

Prereading Activities:

Begin by showing the students the picture on the book cover. Ask students to raise their hands if they have ever had an argument. Choose one student to share the details about the argument and how it was solved. Share one of your experiences if it would be helpful. Create a semantic web to illustrate the types of things we may argue about with different people. After discussing the semantic web, tell students the book you are going to read aloud provides suggestions for avoiding and solving arguments.

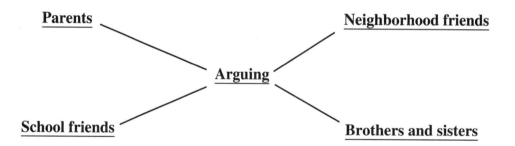

During Reading:

Read the story aloud, stopping periodically to discuss with students. Allow students to apply the I SOLVE strategy.

Postreading/Discussion Questions:

1. When can an argument start?

2. What types of arguments can be harmful?

3. Why would someone want to change the way another person thinks about something?

4. When is it important to talk calmly?

5. Why is a discussion better than an argument?

6. Why is listening to others so important?

7. What are some things you can do to show that you are being a good listener?

8. What are some ways to remind ourselves to think before we speak (e.g., count to 10, take deep breaths)?

9. Why can it be difficult to apologize?

10. Are there times when it is not all right to compromise during an argument?

I SOLVE Strategy

I: Identify the problem presented in the book.

➤ Arguments start when one person does not like what another person has said or done.

S: Solutions to the problem?

a. Book solution: One suggestion the book makes is to talk calmly. Each person should take turns telling how he or she feels.

b. Think about how you feel before you begin to talk, and try not to get angry.

c. Compromise, if needed, to help solve the problem.

d. Other:

O: Obstacles to the solutions?

a. Book solution: The book provides concrete and meaningful solutions for solving arguments. An obstacle would be if one person refused to take turns and continued to interrupt the other.

b. Thinking before talking is difficult if you are angry.

c. If you often argue with the same person, you should not be the only one to compromise.

d. Other:

L: Look at the solutions again and choose one.

Which one could help you in the long run?

V: Validate the solution by trying it.

Try the solution you selected. Solution **a** is one students can try that has few obstacles.

E: Evaluate how the solution worked.

Did the solution work? If not, return to step **S** and select another solution with fewer obstacles.

Extended Learning Activities

1. Problem-Solving Practice Scenario

At home, your two-year-old brother takes your favorite toy. When you try to take it back, he hits you. How can you solve this problem?

I: Identify the problem.

> Your brother will not return your toy, and he hits you.

S: Solutions to the problem?
   a. Tell your parent.
   b. Nicely tell your brother that if he gives you the toy, then you will play with him.
   c. Other:

O: Obstacles to the solutions?
   a. Your parent may help you solve the problem or may tell you to work it out.
   b. Your brother may still not give you the toy even though you asked nicely.
   c. Other:

L: Look at the solutions again and choose one.

Can you work this out, or should you call for your parent?

V: Validate the solution by trying it.

Many times younger siblings take toys because they want our attention.

E: Evaluate how the solution worked.

Did you solve the problem? Why or why not?

2. Reinforcement Activity

Give students a copy of the reinforcement activity "Word Match." Tell students to use the word box to match the word with its definition. When students are finished, they can divide into pairs and quiz each other on the definitions.

Word Match

Directions: Use the word box to match the word with its definition. Think of two additional words that are related to arguments. Write the word and explain the definition using your own words.

apologize	argument	compromise	discussion
ignore	insult	pride	unique

1. _ _ _ _ _ _T   To say something mean to someone.

2. D_ _ _ _ _ _ _ _ _ _ Talking calmly and listening to someone.

3. _ P_ _ _ _ _ _ _ _ To say you are sorry.

4. _ _ _ Q_ _   Something or someone that is one of a kind.

5. _ _ _ _ _ _ _ _ _ E When two people give up part of what they want to come to an agreement.

6. P_ _ _ _   Self-respect that can sometimes get in the way of being fair and reasonable.

7. _ _ _ _ _ _ _ _T When people who do not agree about something get angry at each other.

8. _ _ N_ _ _   To not pay attention to something.

9. _____ _____

10. _____ _____

Football Friends

Title: *Football Friends*
Authors: Jean, Dan, and Dave Marzollo
Copyright: 1997
Publisher: Scholastic
ISBN: 0-590-38395-7
Topic: Fighting with friends
Approximate Grade Levels: 1–3

Book Summary:

Freddy and Mark are friends who love to play football, but each time they play, they end up fighting. With the help of the school principal and his teammates, Freddy learns how to avoid fights and control his anger while playing even better.

Lesson Goal:

To provide students with appropriate alternatives to fighting.

Prereading Activities:

Begin by creating a K-W-L chart with the students about fighting. Let students know there are times when most people feel like fighting but that we stop ourselves before a fight can start. Complete the K section of the chart by filling in what students already know about fighting. Next, complete the W section by asking students what they want to know about fighting and to make predictions about the book. Once you finish the I SOLVE section, complete section L about what the students learned from the book.

During Reading:

Read the book aloud, stopping as needed to clarify issues for students. Before revealing the book's solution, use the I SOLVE strategy. Use the discussion questions if applicable.

Postreading/Discussion Questions:

1. What would have been a better way to decide who picked first?

2. What caused the first fight between Mark and Freddy?

3. How do you think the boys felt after the fight was finished and they were sent to the principal's office?

4. If you were the principal, how would you have handled this situation?

5. How do you think the boys were able to complete Mrs. Smith's homework assignment without fighting?

6. What emotions was Freddy feeling when Mark said he scored a touchdown even though Freddy tagged him?

7. Why did Mark continue to tease Freddy when the two teams lined up?

8. What would you do if you were in the same situation as Freddy?

9. What do you think would have happened if Freddy's teammates had not helped him control his anger?

10. What do you think Mark's reaction would have been once he realized that he could not make Freddy mad and that his team lost the game?

I SOLVE Strategy

Students should understand that talking is the best way to resolve an argument and that it is all right for friends to help you control your anger.

I: Identify the problem presented in the book.

➤ Freddy has a hard time controlling his anger when Mark teases him, and the two boys usually end up physically fighting.

S: Solutions to the problem?

a. Book solution: Mrs. Smith asks the boys to work together and create a roster of two even teams.

b. Book solution: Freddy's team tells him that Mark was only trying to make him mad so he wouldn't play well and that he should ignore Mark and use his anger to run faster.

c. Freddy could have said, "I quit!" and walked away from Mark and the game.

d. Other:

O: Obstacles to the solutions?

a. Book solution: The boys could have argued over how to divide the teams evenly.

b. Book solution: Freddy may have been unable to control his anger, even though his team gave him great suggestions for avoiding a fight.

c. If Freddy quit and walked away, he would have let his team down and probably lost the game.

d. Other:

L: Look at the solutions again and choose one.

Which solution could help you in the long run?

V: Validate the solution by trying it.

Try the solution you selected.

E: Evaluate how the solution worked.

Did the solution work? If not, go back to step **S** and look at the other solutions.

Extended Learning Activities

1. Problem-Solving Practice Scenario

You are at the theater watching a movie, but are bothered by the person in front of you who constantly talks. You gently tap the person on the shoulder and politely ask them to stop talking. The person turns around and says, "Mind your own business, knucklehead!" How can you solve this problem without fighting?

I: Identify the problem.

➤ A person sitting in front of you at the movies will not stop talking, even when you nicely ask them to stop.

S: Solutions to the problem?

a. Immediately get up and go find an employee to come speak to the person.

b. Say to the person, "Be quiet, or else!"

c. Other:

O: Obstacles to the solutions?

a. If you go to find an employee, you will miss part of the movie.

b. If you say something rude to the person, he or she may continue to talk even louder.

c. Other:

L: Look at the solutions again and choose one.

If the person is this rude, consider getting an employee to help you.

V: Validate the solution by trying it.

Even though you may miss a few minutes of the movie, the remainder of the movie will be peaceful.

E: Evaluate how the solution worked.

Congratulate yourself if the solution worked. If it did not work, what other solution is possible?

2. Reinforcement Activity

Give each student a copy of the "Football Friends" letter format. Ask the students to assume the role of Mark and write a letter to Freddy about the game. Students should keep in mind that Mark teased Freddy on purpose to try to make him angry and not play well.

Name:_____ Date:_____

Football Friends

Directions: Imagine you are Mark. Write a letter to Freddy explaining your feelings about the football game.

_____

_____,

_____

_____

_____

_____

_____

_____

_____

_____

_____

_____,

_____

Rainbow Fish and the Big Blue Whale

Title: *Rainbow Fish and the Big Blue Whale*
Author: Marcus Pfister
Copyright: 1998
Publisher: North-South Books
ISBN: 0-7358-1009-5 (trade binding); 0-7358-1010-5 (library binding)
Topic: Fighting
Approximate Grade Levels: 1–3

Book Summary:

Rainbow Fish and his friends are happily living on an ocean reef with plenty of food to eat. One day a large whale swims by the reef and decides to stay. One fish in a bad mood becomes suspicious of the whale and is irritated with him. This fish says things that make the other fish afraid of the whale. The whale feels hurt and angry and decides to teach the other fish a lesson by scaring them. While all the other fish are too afraid of the whale, Rainbow Fish makes peace with the whale by talking out the problem.

Lesson Goal:

To teach students that talking can solve a problem better than fighting.

Prereading Activities:

Begin by discussing the types of things that kids often fight about. Point out to students that many times after a fight or argument is over, we forget the very thing that made us mad. Tell students that is what happened to Rainbow Fish and his friends. Show them the book cover and refresh their memories about how the original *Rainbow Fish* book ended. Tell students this book continues the story.

During Reading:

Read the book aloud, stopping when Rainbow Fish says, "We must make peace with the whale." Have students predict how Rainbow Fish will solve the problem. Use the I SOLVE strategy to create additional solutions.

Postreading/Discussion Questions:

1. How was Rainbow Fish feeling living on the reef?

2. How do you think the fish felt the first time the whale swam by the reef?

3. Why did the whale watch the fish?

4. Why did the author pick the fish with the jagged fins to be in a bad mood?

5. Why would the fish grow suspicious of the whale?

6. Do you think the whale would eat all the krill? Why or why not?

7. Would the whale eat Rainbow Fish and his friends if he ran out of krill to eat?

8. Why did the whale feel hurt at first but then grew angry?

9. Why did Rainbow Fish decide to talk to the whale?

10. What qualities does Rainbow Fish have that are good at solving this problem?

I SOLVE Strategy

Students should understand that talking is the best way to resolve an argument and that it is all right for friends to help you control your anger.

I: Identify the problem presented in the book.

➤ Rainbow Fish and his friends are afraid of the whale because he uses his tail to lash out at the fish.

S: Solutions to the problem?

a. Book solution: Rainbow Fish decides to talk about the problem with the whale to get peace on the reef again.

b. Rainbow Fish could have brought another fish along with him for support as he talked with the whale.

c. The fish could have decided to live in fear of the whale.

d. Other:

O: Obstacles to the solutions?

a. Book solution: The whale could have refused to talk with Rainbow Fish or tried to scare him away.

b. The other fish may not have gone with Rainbow Fish because they were too scared.

c. The fish would have run out of food and the cave was too small.

d. Other:

L: Look at the solutions again and choose one.

Which solution could help you in the long run if someone was fighting with you by trying to intimidate and scare you?

V: Validate the solution by trying it.

Try the solution you think is best.

E: Evaluate how the solution worked.

Did the solution work? If not, go back to step **S** and look at the other solutions.

Extended Learning Activities

1. Problem-Solving Practice Scenario

Pretend you are outside in your front yard playing when a kid bigger than you comes over to you. The bigger kid likes the scooter you are riding and decides to get it by pretending he is going to fight with you. He puts up his fist, shakes it, and says, "Let me ride your scooter or else!" What would you do?

I: Identify the problem.

> ➤ A bigger kid wants to ride your scooter and threatens you by raising his fist.

S: Solutions to the problem?

    a. Drop your scooter and run inside.

    b. Say no to the bigger kid.

    c. Yell for help from an adult or older sibling.

    d. Other:

O: Obstacles to the solutions?

    a. The obstacles to the solutions will vary depending on the circumstances of each individual child. Several solutions may work, so accept many responses from students.

    b. Other:

L: Look at the solutions again and choose one.

Tell students to always avoid a solution that could lead to them getting hurt and to seek immediate assistance from an adult anytime they feel physically threatened.

V: Validate the solution by trying it.

Tell students they would try the solution that promotes peacefully solving the problem.

E: Evaluate how the solution worked.

Remember that physical safety is most important.

2. Reinforcement Activity

Give each student a copy of the reproducible sheet "Fish Talk." Ask students to write about how they would approach and talk with the whale to solve the problem. After students have completed their responses, pair them and allow students to take turns playing the roles of Rainbow Fish and the whale. Students can take turns asking their questions and responding as if they were the big whale. Summarize when the student discussions are completed.

Fish Talk

Directions: Put yourself in the place of Rainbow Fish and pretend that you must talk to the whale. What would you do? What would you say? Answer the following questions about talking to the whale and create some of your own.

1. You are so small compared to the whale. Write how you would act/swim as you approached the whale.

2. The whale is probably still feeling angry and hurt. Write down what you would say first.

3. Write about how you think the whale would respond to what you said. What would you do if the whale tried to scare you again?

4. Write down some of your own ideas to share with the whale.

Additional Readings on Fighting/Arguing

Title and Author: *Let's Talk About Fighting* by Joy Wilt Berry
ISBN: 0-516-02684-4
Approximate Grade Levels: K–2
Copyright: 1984

Book Summary:
    Fighting is described using many examples and colorful illustrations. Suggestions are given for avoiding fights, such as do not play too roughly, stay away from anyone who makes you angry, and ignore anyone who calls you names or says mean things. Solutions include counting to 10, calming down, listening, and compromising.

Title and Author: *Pinky and Rex* by James Howe
ISBN: 0-689-31454-X
Approximate Grade Levels: K–3
Copyright: 1990

Book Summary:
    Pinky and Rex are best friends who take a trip to the museum with Pinky's dad and sister, Amanda. Pinky and Rex both have stuffed animal collections, and in the museum gift shop they both want to buy the same stuffed animal. The two must work out an agreement to solve the argument and still remain friends.

Title and Author: *Let's Be Enemies* by Janice May Udry
ISBN: 0-06-026131-5
Approximate Grade Levels: K–2
Copyright: 1961

Book Summary:
    James and John are friends until James becomes a bossy friend who takes all the crayons, grabs the best digging spoon, and throws sand. Now James is John's enemy, at least until he decides to go over to James's house to tell him some news. By the time he says everything, the boys' strong friendship wins out, and they begin to play again.

Helping Students Understand Anger and Feelings

Chapter 5

Each lesson plan in this chapter can help students learn to identify and express their feelings. Children will also learn strategies for dealing with anger and expressing their anger using appropriate words rather than physical actions.

When Sophie Gets Angry—Really, Really Angry...

Book Title: *When Sophie Gets Angry—Really, Really Angry...*
Author: Molly Bang
Illustrator: Molly Bang
Copyright: 1999
Publisher: Blue Sky Press
ISBN: 0-590-18979-4
Topic: Expressing anger
Approximate Grade Levels: K–2

Book Summary:

Sophie is playing when her sister takes Gorilla away. Sophie gets so angry that she kicks and screams. To calm down, Sophie runs to a special tree where she calms down.

Lesson Goal:

To help students learn how to appropriately express and handle their anger.

Prereading Activities:

Share an example with the class of a time when you were angry. Explain the circumstances and how you handled your anger. Ask the class, "Why do we get angry?" and listen to their responses. Complete a T chart for anger.

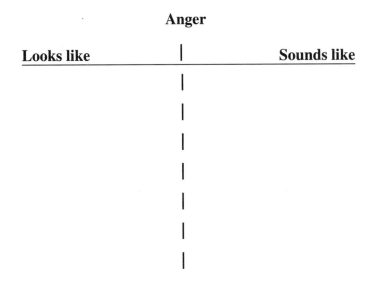

After completing the chart, show students the book cover. Ask them to predict how Sophie will act when she becomes angry and how they think she will handle her anger.

During Reading:

Read the story aloud, allowing time for students to see the illustrations. Before revealing the book's solution, stop and use the I SOLVE strategy with students.

Postreading/Discussion Questions:

1. How do you think Sophie was feeling on the first page when she was busy playing with Gorilla?

2. What happened to make Sophie angry?

3. Looking at the picture of Sophie's face, how can you tell she is angry?

4. Have you ever felt like you wanted to smash the world to smithereens?

5. What does the author mean when she writes, "She roars a red, red roar"?

6. Have you ever felt like a volcano ready to explode?

7. How does running help Sophie?

8. What do you think Sophie thinks about when she is sitting in the old beech tree?

9. How do you act when you get angry?

10. What are some ways you handle your anger?

I SOLVE Strategy

I: Identify the problem presented in the book.

➤ Sophie is angry with her sister.

S: Solutions to the problem?

    a.   Book solution: Sophie runs to her favorite tree and calms down.

    b.   Sophie could have found a safe space in her house to calm down.

    c.   Other:

O: Obstacles to the solutions?

    a.   Book solution: If it were dark outside, Sophie would not be able to run to the tree.

    b.   Sophie may still want to smash things to smithereens in her safe space.

    c.   Other:

L: Look at the solutions again and choose one.

Which one could help you in the long run?

V: Validate the solution by trying it.

Try the solution you selected.

E: Evaluate how the solution worked.

Did it work?

Extended Learning Activities

1. Problem-Solving Practice Scenario

As you are roller skating in your neighborhood, you fall down right in front of a group of kids. You are not hurt, but they laugh at you. How would you feel? What would you do?

I: Identify the problem.

➤ Kids laugh at you when you fall down while roller skating.

S: Solutions to the problem?

    a.   First identify how you feel: angry, embarrassed, or upset. You may decide to say to the kids, "That's not funny. How would you feel?"

    b.   You could laugh, too, and then skate away.

    c.   Other:

O: Obstacles to the solutions?

    a.   The kids may still laugh at you.

    b.   Sometimes it is hard to laugh at ourselves.

    c.   Other:

L: Look at the solutions again and choose one.

Is one solution better than the others? You decide.

V: Validate the solution by trying it.

Practice several solutions during your role playing.

E: Evaluate how the solution worked.

This practice exercise can help you in other situations, too. If one solution did not work, return to step **S** and see if any other solutions might work. Continue with the steps.

2. Reinforcement Activity

Provide students with the page titled "My Angry Face, My Safe Place" or your own piece of drawing paper. Instruct students to draw, on the top half of the page, a picture of their face when they get angry. On the bottom half of the page, they are to draw where they go when they're angry or what they do to calm down. Ask students to write a sentence about each picture.

Name:_____   Date: _____

My Angry Face, My Safe Place

Directions: On the top of the page, draw a picture of your angry face. On the bottom of the page, draw a picture of where you go when you are angry or what you do to calm down.

My Angry Face:

My Safe Place:

When I Feel Angry

Title: *When I Feel Angry*
Author: Cornelia Maude Spelman
Illustrator: Nancy Cote
Copyright: 2000
Publisher: Whitman
ISBN: 0-8075-8888-1
Topic: Expressing anger
Approximate Grade Levels: K–2

Book Summary:

In this book the main character, Rabbit, discusses times when she becomes angry and the different things she does to control her anger, such as taking a deep breath, counting to 10, and getting away from the person who made her angry.

Lesson Goal:

To help students learn how to appropriately express and handle their anger.

Prereading Activities:

Write the word *feelings* on the board and ask students to tell you different types of feelings. As students call out the feelings, categorize them under headings such as "Positive Feelings" and "Angry Feelings." Share a personal example of a time when you had a positive or angry feeling. Ask students to give you examples of times when they had angry feelings. Show them the book cover and ask them to predict what happens.

During Reading:

Read the story aloud and stop before reading the character's solution. Use the I SOLVE strategy.

Postreading/Discussion Questions:

After reading the story, go through it again and ask questions such as the following:

1. Have you ever felt angry when someone made fun of you? Why?

2. How did Rabbit describe the word *anger*?

3. Describe how you feel when you get angry.

4. If you feel angry but don't do anything about it, your anger can't hurt anyone. Why?

5. What are some of the things Rabbit does when she feels angry?

6. How does Rabbit make her anger cooler?

7. What does she mean by the word *cooler*?

8. What types of things make you angry that can't be changed?

9. What may need to change when you feel angry?

10. How can talking and listening make things better?

I SOLVE Strategy

Be sure to reinforce that feeling angry is natural. Anger becomes a problem only when we hurt other people or things.

I: Identify the problem presented in the book.

> ➤ Rabbit feels angry when she has to stop a game to clean up her room, when someone makes fun of her, or when her teacher says she was talking when she wasn't.

S: Solutions to the problem?

   a.   Book solution: Walk away from the person with whom you are angry.

   b.   Book solution: Take deep breaths and blow the air out.

   c.   Book solution: Run or ride a bike.

   d.   Other:

O: Obstacles to the solutions?

   a.   Book solution: Sometimes it is hard to just walk away, or the person may follow you.

   b.   Book solution: You just have to remember to breathe in and out.

   c.   Book solution: You may not feel like exercising.

   d.   Other:

L: Look at the solutions again and choose one.
Which one could help you in the long run?

V: Validate the solution by trying it.
Try the solution you selected.

E: Evaluate how the solution worked.
Did it work?

Extended Learning Activities

1. Problem-Solving Practice Scenario

Imagine you allow a friend to borrow your remote-controlled car. When the friend returns the car, she says, "I'm sorry but I dropped the remote, and now it doesn't work." How would you feel? How would you react?

I: Identify the problem.

➤ Your friend breaks your remote-controlled car.

S: Solutions to the problem?

    a.   Become angry and ask, "How could you do this?"

    b.   Count to 10, take a deep breath, and say, "I'll see if my dad can fix it."

    c.   Other:

O: Obstacles to the solutions?

    a.   The friend may become angry with you and say mean things.

    b.   The friend may offer to replace the remote if your dad cannot fix it.

    c.   Other:

L: Look at the solutions again and choose one.

Which solution would help you calm down and also respect your friend's feelings?

V: Validate the solution by trying it.

Tell students to try the solution during the role play and see how their friend reacted.

E: Evaluate how the solution worked.

If the solution did not work, return to step **S** and evaluate the other solutions. Continue with the steps.

2. Reinforcement Activity

Role-play using the scenarios on the reinforcement sheet, "Get Over It!"

Divide the class into groups of two or three. Two students can participate in the role play, and the third student can be the role-play monitor. The students can take a turn at each role. Students should read the scenario, discuss an appropriate solution, and act it out. Tell students to use different solutions each time they role-play so they get practice with many different responses.

Name:_____   Date: _____

Get Over It!

Directions: Take turns role-playing these scenarios. You should read the scenario, discuss an appropriate solution, and act it out. Remember to use a different solution each time you role-play.

Scenario 1

You are in math class working on multiplication. The teacher asks you to give the answer to one of the problems. When you give the answer, it's not correct. Another student in the class laughs out loud at you. You become angry. What do you do?

Scenario 2

You are at home watching your favorite television show. The show is at the best part when your younger brother comes up and turns off the show. You are furious! What do you do?

Scenario 3

Your family goes on vacation to Disney World. The day you are supposed to go into the Magic Kingdom, it is lightning, thundering, and pouring down rain. You can't believe it and are angry. What do you do?

Scenario 4

You are outside with your best friend and both of you are riding bicycles. You hit a bump and fall off your bike. You are not hurt but your friend laughs at you and calls you a klutz. What do you do?

Remember the solutions from the book? Try some of these during your role play.

- ◆ Book solution (a): Walk away from the person whom you are angry with.

- ◆ Book solution (b): Take deep breaths and blow the air out.

- ◆ Book solution (c): Run or ride a bike.

- ◆ Book solution (d): Rest or cry if it helps.

- ◆ Book solution (e): Ask an adult for help.

Harriet, You'll Drive Me Wild!

Title: *Harriet, You'll Drive Me Wild!*
Author: Mem Fox
Illustrator: Marla Frazee
Copyright: 2000
Publisher: Harcourt
ISBN: 0-15-201977-4
Topic: Expressing anger
Approximate Grade Levels: K–2

Book Summary:

Harriet is a child who does not try to create problems, but she does. She spills juice, drips paint on the carpet, and pulls the tablecloth off the table. Her mother, who does not like to yell and is usually calm, talks to her and Harriet always seems to apologize. Finally, Harriet goes a little too far and her mother gets angry!

Lesson Goal:

To help students learn that adults get angry and to see how they handle their own anger.

Prereading Activities:

Ask students the question "Do adults get angry sometimes, too?" and students will respond yes. You can share an example of a time when you were angry and how you handled your anger appropriately. You also may want to have students share one of their experiences with an angry adult and how the situation was peacefully resolved. Tell students that you are going to read them a story about a girl named Harriet. Show the class the book cover and ask them to predict what happens in the book.

During Reading:

Read the story aloud. Stop reading before the solution is revealed and use the I SOLVE strategy.

Postreading/Discussion Questions:

1. What does the author mean when she says, "Harriet Harris was a *pesky* child"?

2. Have you ever knocked over a glass of juice or milk? What did the adult do or say?

3. Why does Harriet's mother call her a *darling* child when the juice spills?

4. When does Harriet dribble jam on her jeans?

5. How does a person "drive someone wild"? What does that phrase mean?

6. What did Harriet's mother say about the paint?

7. How was Harriet's mother feeling when the tablecloth was pulled off the table?

8. Do you think Harriet's mother is nice or mean? Why?

9. What happened that made Harriet's mom really mad?

10. What happened after Harriet's mom yelled, and what did Harriet and her mom do to make up?

I SOLVE Strategy

Help children realize that adults get angry, too, and that there are things we can do or say to calm down.

I: Identify the problem presented in the book.

> ➤ After a pillow gets ripped open and feathers fly everywhere, Harriet's mother is angry and yells and yells at Harriet.

S: Solutions to the problem?

    a. Book solution: Harriet's mother took a deep breath and said, "I'm sorry."

    b. Her mother could have spoken to her in a calm voice instead of yelling.

    c. Harriet's mother could have laughed and made a joke out of the incident instead of yelling.

    d. Other:

O: Obstacles to the solutions?

    a. Book solution: Taking a deep breath and saying, "I'm sorry" helped everyone calm down and was a better choice than yelling.

    b. It is often hard to speak in a calm voice when we feel so angry inside.

    c. It is hard to laugh and joke when we are angry. Once we calm down a little, it is easier to smile and laugh.

    d. Other:

L: Look at the solutions again and choose one.

Which one could help you in the long run?

V: Validate the solution by trying it.

Try the solution you selected.

E: Evaluate how the solution worked.

Did it work?

Extended Learning Activities

1. Problem-Solving Practice Scenario

At the lunch table, the person sitting next to you spills her juice and it gets your pants all wet. How would you feel? How would you react?

I: Identify the problem.

➤ Your pants are wet because the person sitting next to you spilled her juice.

S: Solutions to the problem?

    a. You may feel angry and jump up and yell, "My pants, my pants!"

    b. Say to yourself, "It's going to be okay," and ask kids around you for napkins.

    c. Other:

O: Obstacles to the solutions?

    a. Even though you are angry, yelling could hurt the other person's feelings.

    b. The kids around you may not have any napkins for drying your pants.

    c. Other:

L: Look at the solutions again and choose one.

Are there other solutions that may be better for drying or replacing your pants?

V: Validate the solution by trying it.

Tell students to role-play the solutions and determine which one works best.

E: Evaluate how the solution worked.

This situation may have happened to someone in the class. Ask their opinion.

2. Reinforcement Activity

Create a picture story map about the events that happened in the book. Give each student a copy of "You Drive Me Wild!" Explain that in the box for part 1, students are to draw something Harriet did to drive her mother wild. The box for part 2 should contain a picture of the pillow exploding or another thing Harriet did to drive her mother wild. In the box for part 3, students are to draw Harriet's mother yelling, and the box for part 4 should be a picture of how they made up. On the back or on a separate sheet of paper, ask students to write a sentence about one thing they can do instead of yelling when they become angry.

Name:_____   Date: _____

You Drive Me Wild!

Directions: Draw four pictures to show what happened
during the story. On the back or on a separate sheet of paper,
write a sentence about one thing you can do instead of
yelling when you become angry.

Part 1

Part 2

Part 3

Part 4

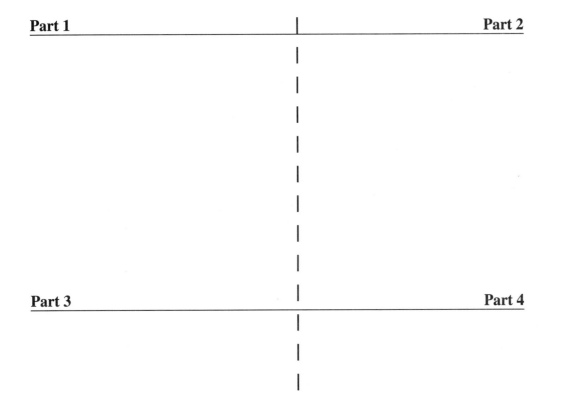

Alexander and the Terrible, Horrible, No Good, Very Bad Day

Title: *Alexander and the Terrible, Horrible, No Good, Very Bad Day*
Author: Judith Viorst
Illustrator: Ray Cruz
Copyright: 1972
Publisher: Atheneum Books for Young Readers
ISBN: 0-689-30072-7
Topic: Expressing feelings appropriately when angry
Approximate Grade Levels: K–3

Book Summary:

This children's classic is about Alexander and his terrible, horrible, no good, very bad day. Everything goes wrong from the moment he gets up until the time he goes to bed. His best friend finds someone to replace him, the shoe store runs out of his size, and his cat won't sleep with him. As he goes to bed, he learns that some days are just like that.

Lesson Goal:

To teach students how to appropriately handle anger.

Prereading Activities:

Ask students if they ever had the kind of day where everything they do turns out wrong. Ask them to share how they felt when everything in their day went wrong. Ask them if other people have days like that, too. Summarize by saying that although we all have bad days sometimes, we just do not want too many of them! Tell students you will read a book about a day in Alexander's life when everything went wrong. Show students the book cover and ask them to predict some of the things that might have gone wrong.

During Reading:

Read the book aloud, stopping as needed to clarify issues for students. Apply the I SOLVE strategy before revealing the book's solution. At the end of the story, you might allow students a minute of individual reflection.

Postreading/Discussion Questions:

1. How was Alexander feeling when he first woke up in the morning? Why?

2. At breakfast time, why did Alexander say he wanted to move to Australia?

3. Where would you go if you were having a terrible, horrible, no good, very bad day?

4. What else could Alexander have done if he was smushed in the car?

5. What would you do if your best friend told you that he or she found another friend?

6. Why weren't people answering Alexander when he told them he was having a terrible, horrible, no good, very bad day?

7. Why didn't Alexander's dad want the family to pick him up anymore?

8. What would you do if you found yourself in some of the same situations as Alexander?

9. Whose fault is it that Alexander had a terrible, horrible, no good, very bad day?

10. Why do you think these things happened to Alexander?

I SOLVE Strategy

Students should understand that everyone has a bad day once in a while, but that there are things you can do to try and improve your day.

I: Identify the problem presented in the book.

Alexander experiences a terrible, horrible, no good, very bad day with many unpleasant happenings.

S: Solutions to the problem?

a. Book solution: Alexander accepts his bad day by sighing and saying, "It's a terrible, horrible, no good, very bad day" and adds that he will move to Australia.

b. Alexander could talk about his feelings with an adult and ask questions about why this is happening to him.

c. Alexander could have stayed home instead of going to many different places.

d. Other:

O: Obstacles to the solutions?

a. Book solution: Alexander would have to convince his parents to move the entire family to Australia.

b. Alexander would need to find an adult with whom he feels comfortable enough to share his feelings.

c. Alexander would miss school and all the other places he had to visit.

d. Other:

L: Look at the solutions again and choose one.

Which one could help you in the long run?

V: Validate the solution by trying it.

Try the solution you selected. Perhaps solution **b**, talking about the problem, would help.

E: Evaluate how the solution worked.

If the first solution did not successfully solve the problem, think about the remaining solutions and their obstacles. Try another solution.

Extended Learning Activities

1. Problem-Solving Practice Scenario

Imagine your cousin borrows one of your favorite shirts to wear. When the shirt is returned, your cousin says, "I'm sorry, but chocolate ice cream spilled on the shirt and the stain won't come out." How would you feel? How would you react?

I: Identify the problem.

➤ Your cousin spilled chocolate ice cream on your favorite shirt, and now it is stained.

S: Solutions to the problem?

    a. You may feel upset and ask your cousin to buy you a new shirt.

    b. Ask your parent to wash the shirt again to try and remove the stain.

    c. Other:

O: Obstacles to the solutions?

    a. Stores may not sell your favorite shirt anymore.

    b. Chocolate is usually a permanent stain.

    c. Other:

L: Look at the solutions again and choose one.

Would you loan anything else to your cousin?

V: Validate the solution by trying it.

Tell students to try the solution that might help both people feel better, such as solution **a**.

E: Evaluate how the solution worked.

Are you still angry? If so, return to step **S** and see if any other solutions might work. Continue with the steps.

2. Reinforcement Activity

Give students a copy of "My Very Bad Day." Tell students to complete the story prompt about their bad day and to illustrate their story by making a card for Alexander to cheer him up. After all students are finished, compile the writings into a class book.

Name:_____ Date: _____

My Very Bad Day

Directions: Complete the story starter about one of your very bad days. When you are finished, create a card that could be used to cheer up Alexander.

My day was bad because _____

_____

_____

_____

_____

_____

_____

_____

_____

_____

_____

Angry Arthur

Title: *Angry Arthur*
Author: Hiawyn Oram
Copyright: 1997
Publisher: Harcourt Brace Jovanovich
ISBN: 0-374-40386-4
Topic: Anger
Approximate Grade Levels: K–2

Book Summary:

Arthur becomes angry when his mother tells him it is time for bed. His anger transforms from being like a thunderstorm all the way to being like an earthquake. He calms down and then wonders why he was ever angry.

Lesson Goal:

To teach students that anger is a normal emotion as well as strategies for coping with anger.

Prereading Activities:

Ask students to name some different emotions. Tell them today's lesson will focus on dealing with anger. Ask if anyone is feeling angry today. Explain that anger is a normal emotion and that there are ways to deal with our anger. Show students the book cover and ask them to predict what happens to Arthur.

During Reading:

Read the book aloud, stopping as needed to clarify issues for students. Toward the end of the book, stop and ask students to predict how Arthur will calm himself. Use the I SOLVE strategy.

Postreading/Discussion Questions:

1. What was Arthur doing when his mom told him it was time for bed?

2. What is a western?

3. Arthur said, "I'll get angry" to his mother. How did he know this?

4. Why would Arthur's mother say, "Get angry"?

5. Do you think his mother knew how angry he would get? Why or why not?

6. Why does anger sometimes make us feel like a dark cloud?

7. Why wouldn't Arthur stop when his mother said, "That's enough"?

8. What did Arthur's father say to him? How did Arthur respond?

9. What do you think Arthur was thinking about while sitting on his bed?

10. Is this story real or pretend?

I SOLVE Strategy

It took Arthur quite a while to calm down. Students can learn many ways to calm themselves quickly.

I: Identify the problem presented in the book.

> ➤ Arthur is angry because he has to go to bed.

S: Solutions to the problem?

    a. Book solution: Find a comfortable place, such as your bed, to relax and think about what is making you angry.

    b. Arthur could have nicely asked his mother to watch television for two more minutes and then gone into bed.

    c. Other:

O: Obstacles to the solutions?

    a. Book solution: Sometimes thinking is not enough to help a person calm down.

    b. His mother may not have agreed to two more minutes of television.

    c. Other:

L: Look at the solutions again and choose one.

Which one could help you in the long run? How can you reach a compromise?

V: Validate the solution by trying it.

Try the solution you selected. Choose a solution that will solve the problem without breaking things.

E: Evaluate how the solution worked.

Were you able to go to bed without becoming angry? If not, talk with your parent about other ways to solve the bedtime blues.

Extended Learning Activities

1.   Problem-Solving Practice Scenario

As you are working on an assignment in school, your pencil lead breaks and causes you to tear your paper. You become so angry at your pencil. What should you do?

I: Identify the problem.

> ➤ When your pencil lead broke, it tore a hole in your paper.

S: Solutions to the problem?

    a. Tell yourself it is okay and get a piece of tape to fix the paper.

    b. Wait for a few minutes to calm down and then get out a new piece of paper to recopy the assignment.

    c. Other:

O: Obstacles to the solutions?

    a. You may stay angry because the hole is too big to fix with tape.

    b. You may be angry because recopying the assignment would take a long time.

    c. Other:

L: Look at the solutions again and choose one.

Which solution would help you calm down the quickest?

V: Validate the solution by trying it.

Tell students to try the solution during their role play.

E: Evaluate how the solution worked.

If the student did not quickly calm down, return to step **S** and see if any other solutions might work. Continue with the steps.

2. Reinforcement Activity

Give each student a copy of the reproducible activity. Instruct students to create a list of the top 10 ways to calm down. Students can work with a partner to create their list. Once students have created their lists, share them with the class. Keep a tally of the top ways students in the class calm themselves. Create a top 10 list for the class.

Top 10 List

Directions: Create a list of the top 10 things you do to calm yourself. Number one on the list is the thing you do the most to calm down.

Example: 1. I like to be alone in my bedroom.

2. I shut my eyes and count to 10.

1. _____

2. _____

3. _____

4. _____

5. _____

6. _____

7. _____

8. _____

9. _____

10. _____

Additional Readings on Anger/Feelings

Title and Author: *When I'm Angry* by Jane Aaron
ISBN: 0-307-44019-2
Approximate Grade Levels: K–3
Copyright: 1998

Book Summary:

Anger is explained in simple terms for children to easily understand. Kids learn that anger is a normal part of life and that there are ways to deal with it appropriately by telling an adult how they feel, acting out their anger with toys, spending time alone, or having something to eat. This book also contains a parent's guide to anger, which teachers may find helpful, too.

Title and Author: *How Do I Feel About Being Angry* by Julie Johnson
ISBN: 0-7613-0910-1
Approximate Grade Levels: K–3
Copyright: 1999

Book Summary:

This book is divided into sections that address the main issues surrounding anger including: the definition of anger, being angry with people and yourself, how being angry makes you feel, hiding other feelings, what to do if someone is angry with you, and dealing with angry feelings. Colorful illustrations and photographs of diverse students are used.

Title and Author: *Every Kid's Guide to Handling Feelings* by Joy Wilt Berry
ISBN: 0-516-01403-X
Approximate Grade Levels: K–3
Copyright: 1987

Book Summary:

Feelings are explained as having a positive or negative influence on one's life depending how you deal with them. This book helps children handle their feelings by discussing what feelings are, what common comfortable and uncomfortable feelings are, and four steps for handling uncomfortable feelings.

Helping to Improve Students' Self-Concept

Young students are vulnerable to the way others perceive them. Teaching students to accept themselves and recognize their strengths is important in developing a positive self-concept. Each lesson plan in this chapter helps teach students to value their character and develop a positive self-concept.

Amazing Grace

Title: *Amazing Grace*
Author: Mary Hoffman
Copyright: 1991
Publisher: Dial Books for Young Readers
ISBN: 0-8037-1040-2
Topic: Self-concept
Approximate Grade Levels: 1–3

Book Summary:
Grace has a great imagination and loves stories and fairy tales. In school her teacher announces that the class is going to present the play *Peter Pan*. Grace wants the role of Peter Pan, but some classmates say she cannot have it because she is black and a girl. With the help of Mom and Nana, Grace learns she can do anything she sets her mind to do.

Lesson Goal:
To help students realize that even if people say we cannot do something, we may if we set our mind to do it.

Prereading Activities:

Ask students the question "What makes each of us different?" Write their responses on the board. After writing the responses, indicate that no one has all the listed characteristics. Discuss the different characteristics as well as the similarities among us. Conclude by stating, "As people we each have strengths, such as musical, athletic, or academic talents, that make us unique, and we also share many similarities with others."

During Reading:

Read the book aloud. Before revealing if Grace earned the part of Peter Pan, stop and use the I SOLVE strategy to predict how she would react if she did not earn the part. Use the discussion questions if applicable.

Postreading/Discussion Questions:

1. What does the author mean when she says Grace loved stories "out of Nana's long memory"?

2. What were some of the parts Grace liked to play when she acted out her stories?

3. How do you think Grace felt as she acted out the different stories?

4. What would Grace do when there was no one else around to play with?

5. How were Mom and Nana's lives in Grace's hands?

6. What do you think Grace said to Raj when he said she could not play Peter Pan?

7. Why was Grace feeling sad when she came home from school?

8. What does it mean to "put your mind to it"?

9. What did Grace learn from seeing the ballet?

10. Do you think it was easy for Grace to earn the part of Peter Pan? Why?

I SOLVE Strategy

I: Identify the problem presented in the book.

➤ Grace is unsure if she can earn the part of Peter Pan in the class play.

S: Solutions to the problem?

   a. Book solution: By setting her mind to practicing hard, learning all the words, and believing in herself, Grace's hard work paid off and she earned the Peter Pan part.

   b. Other:

O: Obstacles to the solutions?

   a. Book solution: Grace may practice hard, learn the words, and believe in herself and still not earn the part of Peter Pan. She may feel sad, but at least she knows she tried her hardest.

   b. Other:

L: Look at the solutions again and choose one.

Which one could help you if you did not earn the part you wanted?

V: Validate the solution by trying it.

Try the solution you selected.

E: Evaluate how the solution worked.

If you earned the part, then the problem is solved. How would you react if you did not earn the part? Review the solutions in step **S**.

Extended Learning Activities

1. Problem-Solving Practice Scenario

Imagine you have the starring role in the class play. During the first performance, you forget some of the words to say. What would you do?

I: Identify the problem.

➤ During the class play you forget the words to say.

S: Solutions to the problem?

    a. Run off the stage crying.

    b. Make up your own words to keep the play going.

    c. Other:

O: Obstacles to the solutions?

    a. Since you are the star, running off the stage may ruin the play.

    b. Making up your own words may help you remember the right words.

    c. Other:

L: Look at the solutions again and choose one.

Choose the solution that would solve the problem and help you feel good.

V: Validate the solution by trying it.

Practice all the possible solutions during the role play.

E: Evaluate how the solution worked.

If the solution did not solve the problem, return to step **S** and see if any other solutions might work. Continue with the steps.

2. Reinforcement Activity

Divide students into groups of three. Give each group a copy of the play script for "Ruler for a Day." Tell each group they are going to be acting out the words for the play. The group will have to use the information they learned from the I SOLVE activity to choose who plays the lead role of the ruler. After each group decides who acts out each part, allow them to practice. Each group can perform their skit for the class.

Ruler for a Day

Directions: In groups, use the I SOLVE strategy to decide who will play the part of the Ruler, Assistant 1, and Assistant 2. Practice the skit by reading the parts. After practicing, prepare to act out your skit.

Ruler: "What, what, what happened? I was sitting in school at my desk when all of a sudden I saw a flash. Where am I and who are you?"

Assistant 1: "I am your assistant. You are Ruler for the day, Your Majesty."

Assistant 2: "Yes, anything you want is at your command. You are the Ruler of this village."

Ruler: "Really, I am *the* Ruler? The Ruler? Oh boy, this is going to be fun."

Assistant 1: "What would you like to do first Your Majesty?"

Ruler: "Well, let's see. Why don't I decide that we can watch television all day."

Assistant 2: "What is television Your Majesty?"

Ruler: "Television, you don't know what television is? Haven't you heard of cartoons, movies, music television, and TV games? They're the best!"

Assistant 1: "No, you are a ruler of a village where there is no television."

Assistant 2: "No television here."

Ruler: "How can this be? I am the Ruler! I am in charge! I make the rules!"

Assistant 1: "Well you see, even the Ruler has rules, Your Majesty."

Assistant 2: "Yes, rules for the Ruler."

Ruler: "Ahhh, I must be dreaming because if *I* am the Ruler then I have the power to make the rules and I say we watch television and play TV games. I am going to count to three and there had better be a television in front of me by the time I reach three. One, two, three!"

Assistant 1: "What are you doing friend?"

Assistant 2: "Yeah, you must have been day dreaming or something because it's time for lunch. Close your book and line-up."

Ruler: "Was this a dream? It seemed so real! I guess that's why I was only Ruler for a day!"

Ignis

Title: *Ignis*
Author: Gina Wilson
Copyright: 2001
Publisher: Candlewick Press
ISBN: 0-7636-1623-0
Topic: Self-concept
Approximate Grade Levels: 1–3

Book Summary:

Ignis is a young dragon who wants to be like all the other dragons and blow fire, but he cannot. He searches for places where he might find his fire and become like everyone else.

Lesson Goal:

To help students identify that we all want to fit in and be accepted by others.

Prereading Activities:

Show students the book cover and ask them to make predictions about the content. Ask students what they would do if everyone in the class wore a red shirt and they were wearing a blue shirt. How would they feel? Tell them this book is about a dragon who wants to be like everyone else.

During Reading:

Read the book aloud. Before revealing if Ignis found his fire, stop and use the I SOLVE strategy to predict the outcome. Use the discussion questions if applicable.

Postreading/Discussion Questions:

1. What strengths did Ignis have?

2. Even though Ignis had strengths, why was he sad?

3. How did Ignis feel when he could not play dragon games?

4. Why did Scintilla still love Ignis?

5. Why did Cara think Ignis was beautiful and not a monster?

6. Why did Ignis decide to stay with Cara for a week?

7. What would be great about being a dragon?

8. Why did Ignis and Cara become such good friends?

9. What does it mean when Ignis's heart felt fiery?

10. What was Ignis feeling when he returned to Dragonland?

I SOLVE Strategy

I: Identify the problem presented in the book.

➤ Ignis, the dragon, is unable to blow fire like the other dragons.

S: Solutions to the problem?

a. Book solution: Ignis went off by himself to try and find his fire. By having some time to think and learn about himself, Ignis was able to find his fire.

b. Ignis could have remained in the village and accepted that, in time, he would find his fire.

c. Other:

O: Obstacles to the solutions?

a. Book solution: When Ignis went off by himself, his family and the older dragons were worried about him. He should have told someone his plan.

b. By waiting, Ignis felt he was different from everyone else and that he did not fit in.

c. Other:

L: Look at the solutions again and choose one.

Which one could help you if you felt like you did not fit in?

V: Validate the solution by trying it.

Try role-playing the solution you selected.

E: Evaluate how the solution worked.

Did the solution help you feel good about yourself? If not, review the solutions again in step **S** and decide whether to choose another one.

Extended Learning Activities

1. Problem-Solving Practice Scenario

Pretend you cannot ride a two-wheel bicycle, but your two best friends who are your same age can. You practice and try hard but are unable to ride and feel frustrated. How could you solve this problem?

I: Identify the problem.

  ➤ You are unable to ride a two-wheel bicycle.

S: Solutions to the problem?

  a. Ask your friends to help you learn to ride.

  b. Give up and wait until after your next birthday to try and ride a two-wheeler.

  c. Other:

O: Obstacles to the solutions?

  a. Your friends may say, "No."

  b. When waiting until your next birthday, you miss opportunities to ride with friends.

  c. Other:

L: Look at the solutions again and choose one.

  Choose the solution that would solve the problem and help you feel good.

V: Validate the solution by trying it.

  Practice all the possible solutions during the role play.

E: Evaluate how the solution worked.

  If the solution did not solve the problem, return to step **S** and see if any other solutions might work. Continue with the steps.

2. Reinforcement Activity

Give each student a copy of "Badge of Honor" to complete. Tell students that in each of the four sections, they should draw a picture representing one of their strengths. After completing the picture, students can write a sentence or individual words about their drawing.

Name:_____   Date: _____

Badge of Honor

Directions: In each area draw a picture representing your strengths or talents. On a separate sheet of paper, write a sentence about each picture.

The Tower

Title: *The Tower*
Author: Richard Paul Evans
Copyright: 2001
Publisher: Simon & Schuster
ISBN: 0-689-83467-5
Topic: Self-concept
Approximate Grade Levels: 2–3

Book Summary:

A man who wants to be great visits an old wise man, who tells him that others must look up to him. The man builds himself a tall tower so that all others must look up to him, only to realize that it is lonely at the top. One day a passing bird tells the man of an old woman greater than he. The man goes to meet her and finds the truth in the saying "To be great is not to be higher than another, but to lift another higher."

Lesson Goal:

To help students realize that when we help others, it helps us feel good about ourselves.

Prereading Activities:

Begin a class discussion by asking students the question "How does a person become great?" Write students' responses on the board, organized as a brainstorm. Tell students the book you are going to read is about a young man who tries to answer this question. Show them the book's cover and tell students to listen carefully to see if their predictions for the story came true.

During Reading:

Read the book aloud. Before revealing if the young man decided to follow the old woman's advice, stop and use the I SOLVE strategy to predict how he will act on her advice.

Postreading/Discussion Questions:

1. Do you think the old man gave the young man correct advice about how to become great?
2. Did the old man mean the young man should build a platform or tower to stand on in order to become great?
3. How do you think the young man was feeling as he built his tower?
4. What does the author mean when he says, "A great man must often walk alone"?
5. Do you think the bird was correct when he said that from the ground, the young man looked small to the villagers?
6. How could the young man's tower fall?
7. Why did the bird tell the young man about the old woman?
8. Why does the old woman pity the young man in the tower?
9. What does the old woman mean when she says, "To be great is not to be higher than another, but to lift another higher"?
10. Why did the village people finally recognize the young man as being great?

I SOLVE Strategy

I: Identify the problem presented in the book.

➤ The young man does not know how to become a great man.

S: Solutions to the problem?

    a. Book solution: The young man realized that sitting in a tower high above others did not make him great, so he knocked down the tower and gave others its wood.

    b. The young man could have sought advice from other village people about becoming great instead of just asking the wise old man.

    c. Other:

O: Obstacles to the solutions?

    a. Book solution: By knocking down his tower, the young man could have been regarded as a quitter, since he decided to become a villager again.

L: Look at the solutions again and choose one.

If you wanted to become a great person, which solution seems best?

V: Validate the solution by trying it.

Try the solution you selected and role-play it with a friend.

E: Evaluate how the solution worked.

Did you feel great by helping others? If not, review the solutions in step **S** and consider trying another alternative.

Extended Learning Activities

1. Problem-Solving Practice Scenario

> Imagine you want to become the best dancer, so you practice hard every day. You practice your dance routine to perfection and perform in a big show. Even though you dance perfectly, someone boos at you when you finish. What would you do?

I: Identify the problem.

➤ Someone boos at your dancing.

S: Solutions to the problem?

    a.   Ignore the person and continue to smile.

    b.   Yell at the person for booing and call him or her a name.

    c.   Other:

O: Obstacles to the solutions?

    a.   When just ignoring the person, you run the risk of the person booing at you again.

    b.   Yelling at the person would make you look small and insecure instead of great.

    c.   Other:

L: Look at the solutions again and choose one.

Choose the solution that would make you the greater person.

V: Validate the solution by trying it.

Practice all the possible solutions during the role play.

E: Evaluate how the solution worked.

Which solution looks like it could produce positive results? If needed, return to step **S** and see if any other solutions might work. Continue with the steps.

2.   Reinforcement Activity

Provide each student with a copy of "A Great Idea." Explain that when we do nice things for others, it helps us to feel great about ourselves, and then people view us as great. Tell students that in each section of the paper, they should write down at least one idea of something they could do to help others feel great. In turn, the act of kindness will help others to view them as a great person or student.

A Great Idea

Directions: In each section, write at least one idea about a kind act you could do to help others feel great. By doing kind things, others will see you as a great person.

During School   At Home

Playing with Friends   At a Store

I Love My Hair!

Title: *I Love My Hair!*
Author: Natasha Anastasia Tarpley
Copyright: 1998
Publisher: Little, Brown
ISBN: 0-316-52275-9 (hardcover); 0-316-52375-5 (paperback)
Topic: Self-concept
Approximate Grade Levels: 1–3

Book Summary:

Keyana, a young African-American girl, describes her beautiful hair and the different styles she can wear. One day Keyana is teased about her hair during school, and her teacher tells her that wearing an Afro was a way people stood up for what they believed.

Lesson Goal:

To help students realize that although people have different physical features, we each should be proud of our looks.

Prereading Activities:

Ask students to look around the room at their classmates' hair. Point out that each person's hair is a little different. Some hair is a different color, length, or texture; others may have a little or a lot of hair. Tell students the book you are going to read is about a girl and the reasons why she loves her hair.

During Reading:

Read the book aloud. Before revealing how Keyana solves the problem about being teased, stop and use the I SOLVE strategy to predict her solution. Use the discussion questions if applicable.

Postreading/Discussion Questions:

1. What does Keyana have done every night before bed?

2. How do you respond when your hair is pulled while being brushed?

3. Which style of hair do you think Keyana likes best?

4. How do the beads in Keyana's hair help her remember things to buy?

5. How is Keyana feeling as she goes to the store? Why?

6. Why did kids tease Keyana?

7. How was Keyana feeling when she let her head hang down low? Why?

8. What lesson did Keyana's teacher teach?

9. Why does Keyana feel like she can fly?

10. What are some words you would use to describe Keyana's hair?

I SOLVE Strategy

I: Identify the problem presented in the book.

> ➤ Keyana loves her hair, but one day at school she is teased about the way her hair looks.

S: Solutions to the problem?

    a. Book solution: Keyana's teacher made her feel better by telling a story about the meaning of wearing an Afro.

    b. Keyana could have stayed sad and let the kids' comments ruin her day.

    c. Other:

O: Obstacles to the solutions?

    a. Book solution: Kids still might tease Keyana even though they understand the meaning of wearing an Afro.

    b. By staying sad, Keyana would have let the mean kids get what they wanted: to hurt her feelings.

    c. Other:

L: Look at the solutions again and choose one.

Which solution could help if you loved your hair but kids teased you?

V: Validate the solution by trying it.

Try the solution that would keep you feeling good about your hair and stop the teasing.

E: Evaluate how the solution worked.

Did the solution work and keep you feeling good about your hair and solve the problem? If not, review the solutions in step **S** and continue with the remaining steps.

Extended Learning Activities

1. Problem-Solving Practice Scenario

Imagine you are with your friends getting ready to play a game of kick ball. All the kids are getting chosen except you. Finally, you are the last person to be picked for someone's team. How would you feel? What could you do?

I: Identify the problem.

> ➤ You are the last one picked for the kick ball game.

S: Solutions to the problem?

    a.   Say to yourself, "It is no big deal. Someone had to be last. I'm still a good player."

    b.   Shout in a loud voice, "Why am I the last one picked? Don't you think I am any good at this game?" Then look mad and leave really fast.

    c.   Other:

O: Obstacles to the solutions?

    a.   Even though these positive words are what you want to say to yourself, it may be hard if you are feeling hurt and upset.

    b.   Shouting and leaving the game may make you look foolish and would let the team down.

    c.   Other:

L: Look at the solutions again and choose one.

Choose the solution that would solve the problem and make you look confident.

V: Validate the solution by trying it.

Practice all the possible solutions during the role-play activity.

E: Evaluate how the solution worked.

If the solution did not solve the problem, return to step **S** and see if any other solutions might work. Continue with the steps.

2. Reinforcement Activity

Give each student a copy of "I Love My _____." Explain to students that each person has particular features or things they really love about themselves. On the top half of the paper, students should write or draw about their own features they love the most. On the bottom half of the paper, students should choose a person they love and write or draw what they love most about that person. Share if time permits.

Name:_____ Date: _____

I Love My _____ .

Directions: On the top half of the paper, write or draw about your features you love the most. On the bottom half of the paper, choose a person you love and write or draw what you love most about that person.

Myself

Someone I Love

Chrysanthemum

Title: *Chrysanthemum*
Author: Kevin Henkes
Copyright: 1991
Publisher: Dial Books for Young Readers
ISBN: 0-8037-1040-2
Topic: Self-concept
Approximate Grade Levels: 2–3

Book Summary:

Chrysanthemum is a girl who loves everything about her name until she starts school and others make fun of her.

Lesson Goal:

To help students recognize that if people make fun of us, they are usually trying to make themselves feel powerful, but if we peacefully solve the problem, the power remains with us.

Prereading Activities:

Ask students to raise their hands and say what they like most about themselves. Explain that everyone has certain characteristics they like most about themselves. After writing students' ideas on the board, tell them that the story you are going to read is about a girl who loves her name. Ask students to guess the name. When they cannot guess the girl's name, tell them it is Chrysanthemum. Notice students' responses. Did they laugh or snicker? If so, explain that their reaction to Chrysanthemum's name was a put-down and that it would hurt her feelings. Tell students to notice how the characters in the story react to Chrysanthemum's name.

During Reading:

Read the book aloud. Before revealing how Chrysanthemum solved the teasing, stop and use the I SOLVE strategy to predict potential solutions. Discuss the story using the discussion questions if applicable.

Postreading/Discussion Questions:

1. How did Chrysanthemum feel about her name?

2. How do you think Chrysanthemum felt about herself?

3. What do you think happens when Chrysanthemum starts school?

4. How did Chrysanthemum feel when everyone giggled upon hearing her name? Why?

5. What does it mean when the author says, "Chrysanthemum wilted"?

6. Do you think Chrysanthemum should change her name?

7. What did Chrysanthemum's parents do to help her feel better?

8. Do you think Chrysanthemum's parents were right when they said the other kids were just jealous of her name?

9. Why was Chrysanthemum's dream such a nightmare?

10. How did Chrysanthemum feel after hearing Mrs. Twinkle's name? Why?

I SOLVE Strategy

I: Identify the problem presented in the book.

> ➤ Chrysanthemum does not feel good about herself because she is teased about her name.

S: Solutions to the problem?

    a. Book solution: Chrysanthemum's music teacher says she loves her name and is considering naming her baby girl Chrysanthemum.

    b. Chrysanthemum could have told the other students in the class to stop making fun of her name and that her feelings were hurt.

    c. Other:

O: Obstacles to the solutions?

    a. Book solution: There may not always be a teacher who says he or she loves your name.

    b. It is possible that even though Chrysanthemum tells students how she is feeling, they could continue to tease her.

    c. Other:

L: Look at the solutions again and choose one.

Which one could help you feel better about yourself if kids were making fun of your name?

V: Validate the solution by trying it.

Practice each possible solution as you role-play with your classmates.

E: Evaluate how the solution worked.

Remember to choose a solution that will help you feel good about yourself as well as solve the problem. If the solution did not solve the problem, return to step **S** and see if any other solutions might work. Continue with the steps.

Extended Learning Activities

1. Problem-Solving Practice Scenario

Imagine you are on a baseball or softball team. During your last two times up to bat, you strike out. When it is your third turn up to bat, you strike out again. You feel like you let your team down and are considering quitting. What should you do to get your confidence back?

I: Identify the problem.

➤ You feel like you let the team down when you struck out.

S: Solutions to the problem?

a. Quit the team.

b. Practice harder so that you will improve and feel better about yourself.

c. Other:

O: Obstacles to the solutions?

a. Quitting the team would not help you feel better about yourself.

b. Practicing may or may not help you improve.

c. Other:

L: Look at the solutions again and choose one.

Choose the solution that would solve the problem and help you regain your confidence.

V: Validate the solution by trying it.

Practice each possible solution as you role-play with your classmates.

E: Evaluate how the solution worked.

Remember to choose a solution that helps you improve your game and helps you feel good about yourself. If the solution did not solve the problem, return to step **S** and see if any other solutions might work. Continue with the steps.

2. Reinforcement Activity

Give each student a copy of the reproducible activity "Exciting Names." Tell students they are to write each letter of their name vertically down the left side of the paper. Using each letter, students should write a sentence that describes their positive characteristics. For example:

E Easy to get along with

M Makes people laugh

I Is good at reading

L Loves swimming

Y Yellow is her favorite color

Exciting Names

Directions: Write your name in CAPITAL letters down ↓ the left side of the paper. Using each letter, write a sentence that describes positive things about you. For example:

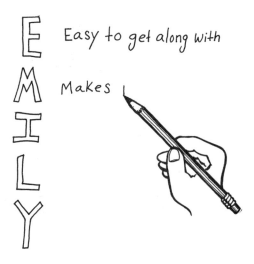

E   Easy to get along with

M   Makes people laugh

I   Is good at reading

L   Loves swimming

Y   Yellow is her favorite color

Additional Readings on Improving Self-Concept

Title and Author: *Stand Tall, Molly Lou Melon* by Patty Lovell
ISBN: 0-399-23416-0
Approximate Grade Levels: K–3
Copyright: 2001

Book Summary:
> Even though Molly Lou Melon is short and clumsy, has buck teeth, and has a voice that sounds like a bullfrog, she feels good about herself. Her grandmother's advice is to walk proud, smile big, and sing loud. Molly Lou does not feel so good when she starts a new school and a bully picks on her, but she knows how to handle him.

Title and Author: *A Valentine for Norman Noggs* by Valiska Gregory
ISBN: 0-06-027657-6
Approximate Grade Levels: K–3
Copyright: 1999

Book Summary:
> Norman Noggs likes a new girl in his class, but two other boys like her, too. Norman feels insecure and does not know if the new girl will like him because one boy is the strongest boy in the class and the other is the biggest boy in the class. Norman decides to make her a valentine but is worried she will not like him. Norman's confidence rises when she gives him a valentine, too.

Title and Author: *The Treasure Hunt* by Bill Cosby
ISBN: 0-590-95618-3
Approximate Grade Levels: K–3
Copyright: 1997

Book Summary:
> Everyone in Little Bill's family has a special treasure they value and care about. Little Bill is feeling down because he does not think he has anything special to treasure. He searches his room and finds rocks, crayons, and clothes but no treasure. While searching, Little Bill's great-grandmother enters his room and asks him to tell her a story. By telling her a story, Little Bill begins to feel better and realizes his treasures are his family and his ability to make people laugh.

Chapter 7

Helping Students Understand Disabilities

Approximately 6 to 10 percent of school-age students have a disability. The majority of students with disabilities are in general education classrooms for part of the school day. Each lesson plan from this chapter helps others develop an awareness and understanding of individuals with disabilities.

Hooway for Wodney Wat

Title: *Hooway for Wodney Wat*
Author: Helen Lester
Copyright: 1999
Publisher: Houghton Mifflin
ISBN: 0-395-92392-1
Topic: Speech disability
Approximate Grade Levels: 2–3

Book Summary:

Rodney Rat cannot pronounce his *r*'s, and the other rodents tease him. When Rodney is able to get rid of a class bully, Camilla Capybera, the teasing stops, and Rodney feels good about himself and becomes the class hero.

Lesson Goal:

To help students learn that a person with a speech disorder is just like everyone else.

Prereading Activities:

Begin by telling students you are going to share a book with them about something that affects many children: speech problems. Explain that when people have a speech problem, they may feel self-conscious or uncomfortable speaking around others. Tell them the book you are going to read is about a mouse with a speech problem and how he learned to feel good about himself.

During Reading:

Read the book aloud. Before revealing how Rodney solved the problem with Camilla, stop and use the I SOLVE strategy to predict potential solutions. Discuss the story using the discussion questions if applicable.

Postreading/Discussion Questions:

1. What is a rodent?

2. Why did Rodney answer the kids' questions if he knew they would laugh at him?

3. How was Rodney feeling when he hid inside his jacket?

4. What do you think will happen with Camilla in the class?

5. What did Camilla do to prove she was smart?

6. Why would the other rodents feel uncomfortable with Camilla in the class?

7. Do you think Rodney felt excited when the teacher picked his name to lead Simon Says? Why?

8. What was Camilla supposed to do instead of pulling up weeds during the game?

9. Why did Rodney's voice become stronger?

10. Why did Rodney feel so much better at the end of the story?

I SOLVE Strategy

I: Identify the problem presented in the book.

➤ Rodney is teased because of his speech disorder.

S: Solutions to the problem?

a. Book solution: Rodney gains confidence when he becomes the leader of a Simon Says game and solves the problem with a class bully.

b. Rodney could have told the other students in the class to stop teasing him and that he could not help his speech disorder.

c. Other:

O: Obstacles to the solutions?

    a.   Book solution: Camilla still could have made fun of Rodney as he led the game.

    b.   It is possible that even though Rodney tells students how he feels, they may continue to tease him.

    c.   Other:

L: Look at the solutions again and choose one.

Which solution can help you solve the problem if you have a speech disorder?

V: Validate the solution by trying it.

Role-play the possible solutions and determine which one is best to try first.

E: Evaluate how the solution worked.

Remember to choose a solution that will help you feel good about yourself as well as solve the problem. If the solution did not solve the problem, return to step **S** and see if any other solutions might work. Continue with the steps.

Extended Learning Activities

1. Problem-Solving Practice Scenario

> Imagine some kids tease you about your new haircut and it makes you feel bad. What should you do to solve this problem?

I: Identify the problem.

    ➤ Kids are teasing you because of a new haircut.

S: Solutions to the problem?

    a.   Tell them to stop and explain that everyone gets haircuts.

    b.   Explain the situation to an adult and enlist their support in solving the problem.

    c.   Other:

O: Obstacles to the solutions?

    a.   Telling the students to stop may not work if they do not respect your feelings.

    b.   An adult may help you solve the problem, but then you are not solving it yourself.

    c.   Other:

L: Look at the solutions again and choose one.

Choose the solution that would solve the problem and help you feel accepted.

V: Validate the solution by trying it.

Practice each possible solution as you role-play with your classmates.

E: Evaluate how the solution worked.

If the solution helped you solve the problem, you are satisfied. If not, return to step **S** and review the remaining solutions and possible outcomes.

2. Reinforcement Activity

Give each student a copy of the lesson reaction sheet. Tell students to put themselves in Rodney's place and imagine they have a speech disorder. They should answer the questions to think about how to react to a person with a speech disorder.

How Would You React?

Directions: Imagine you are Rodney. Put yourself in his place and think about how he feels when kids laugh at him. Answer each question as if you were Rodney.

1. I feel miserable when kids laugh at my speech. What could I tell them to help them understand my problem?

2. In order to show the other kids what a speech disorder is like, try this. Stick out your tongue. Hold it with your thumb and pointer finger as you try to say these sentences:
   a. Let's go out and play.
   b. Saturday is my favorite day of the week.
   c. I would like to eat macaroni and cheese for dinner tonight.

3. How did it feel when you tried to talk while holding your tongue?

4. How did you sound when you held your tongue?

5. What would it be like to talk like this all the time? Explain your answer.

Thank You, Mr. Falker

Title: *Thank You, Mr. Falker*
Author: Patricia Polacco
Copyright: 1998
Publisher: Philomel
ISBN: 0-399-23737-2
Topic: Learning disabilities
Approximate Grade Levels: 1–3

Book Summary:

Trisha is a young girl who loves books but has difficulty reading them until fifth grade when a special teacher, Mr. Falker, teaches her to overcome her reading problem. This book is based on the author's real-life experience of learning to read.

Lesson Goal:

To help students realize that many people have difficulty reading even though they try very hard and that often with special instruction, people learn to read.

Prereading Activities:

Explain the book you will read today is a true story about a young girl who tries very hard to read but has difficulty. Tell students that some people see the letters and words, but often they appear mixed up or even backward. When this happens, it makes learning to read very difficult. Tell students that with special help, these kids learn to read, too.

During Reading:

Read the book aloud. Before revealing how Trisha learns to read, use the I SOLVE strategy to predict potential solutions. Discuss the story using the discussion questions if applicable.

Postreading/Discussion Questions:

1. Why did Trisha's family pour honey on books?
2. What is Trisha good at doing?
3. Why did Trisha feel different in first grade?
4. Is it all right to be different? Why?
5. How did Grandma help Trisha?
6. Why would boys call her "dummy" in her new school?
7. What did Mr. Falker do to stand up for Trisha?
8. Why did Trisha begin to believe the other students?
9. How did Mr. Falker know that Trisha felt lonely and afraid?
10. What made Trisha feel better about herself?

I SOLVE Strategy

I: Identify the problem presented in the book.

➤ Trisha has difficulty learning to read.

S: Solutions to the problem?

    a. Book solution: Trisha had a teacher who understood her problem reading and knew how to get her help.

    b. Trisha could have approached her teacher and asked for extra help learning to read.

    c. Other:

O: Obstacles to the solutions?

    a. Book solution: Trisha had to wait a long time to finally get a teacher who could help her overcome her reading difficulty.

    b. Trisha could have been too embarrassed or scared to ask her teacher for extra help.

    c. Other:

L: Look at the solutions again and choose one.

Which one could help you feel better about yourself and improve your reading?

V: Validate the solution by trying it.

Be persistent; if one solution does not work, try another.

E: Evaluate how the solution worked.

Tell students, "Choose a solution that will help you feel good about yourself and stop others from teasing you as well as help you learn to read. Anytime you do not understand something or have difficulty, talk to the teacher right away." This problem requires adult intervention.

Extended Learning Activities

1. Problem-Solving Practice Scenario

Imagine your parents just told you they are moving to Mexico, and you do not speak any Spanish. You need to learn to speak and read Spanish when you arrive. What should you do?

I: Identify the problem.

> ➤ You do not know how to speak Spanish.

S: Solutions to the problem?

    a.   Ask your parents to hire a tutor for you.

    b.   Refuse to move to Mexico with your parents.

    c.   Other:

O: Obstacles to the solutions?

    a.   Hiring a tutor is expensive.

    b.   Refusing to move to Mexico would leave you without your family.

    c.   Other:

L: Look at the solutions again and choose one.

Choose the solution that would solve the problem and create a win-win situation for everyone.

V: Validate the solution by trying it.

Practice each possible solution as you role-play with your classmates.

E: Evaluate how the solution worked.

Which solution is best for reaching a compromise and solving this problem?

2. Reinforcement Activity

Ask students if they have ever created a secret code. Tell students reading is also a code and explain that when we create a code, only the people who know the code can read the message. Ask students to decipher the secret code on the reproducible activity sheet as well as create their own secret message.

Secret Code

Directions: Use the code to read the secret message. Is it hard to read using a new code?

Code								
1 = a	2 = b	3 = c	4 = d	5 = e	6 = f	7 = g	8 = h	9 = i
10 = j	11 = k	12 = l	13 = m	14 = n	15 = o	16 = p	17 = q	18 = r
19 = s	20 = t	21 = u	22 = v	23 = w	24 = x	25 = y	26 = z	

Secret Message

16 5 20 5 18   16 9 16 5 18   16 9 3 11 5 4   1   16 5 3 11   15 6

_____   _____   _____   ___   _____   _____

16 9 3 11 5 12 5 4   16 5 16 16 5 18 19

_____   _____ .

Now use the code to create your own secret message.

_____

_____

_____

Way to Go, Alex!

Title: *Way to Go, Alex!*
Author: Robin Tulver
Copyright: 1999
Publisher: Whitman
ISBN: 0-8075-1583-3
Topic: Mental disabilities
Approximate Grade Levels: K–3

Book Summary:

Carly's older brother is mentally disabled. She learns to focus on her brother's abilities, not his disabilities, as she helps him prepare for the Special Olympics.

Lesson Goal:

To help students learn to focus on a person's abilities rather than disabilities.

Prereading Activities:

Ask students to raise their hands if they know anything about the Olympics. Write students' responses on the board. Now ask people to raise their hands if they know anything about the Special Olympics. Write down students' responses. Provide additional information about the Special Olympics. Tell students today's book is about a sister and brother as they prepare for the Special Olympics.

During Reading:

Read the book aloud. Before revealing if Alex wins any medals, stop and use the I SOLVE strategy to predict the outcome. After reading, discuss the story using the discussion questions.

Postreading/Discussion Questions:

1. Why isn't Carly happy for Annie's brother?

2. How are Carly's and Annie's families different?

3. Can Carly's invention help Alex?

4. How does Carly help Alex get ready for the Special Olympics?

5. How does Carly feel when she helps Alex practice?

6. Is it all right if Carly thinks things that aren't nice about Alex?

7. What is the Special Olympics oath?

8. Why would Alex stop running at the ribbon?

9. Why does Carly want to go home after the softball throw?

10. What does Carly realize at the end of the book?

I SOLVE Strategy

I: Identify the problem presented in the book.

➤ Carly would like her brother to be like other kids without disabilities.

S: Solutions to the problem?
   a. Book solution: After her brother competes in the Special Olympics, Carly learns that her brother tries hard and is a wonderful person.
   b. Carly could talk with her parents about her brother Alex's disability.
   c. Other:

O: Obstacles to the solutions?
   a. Book solution: Not all individuals with disabilities compete in the Special Olympics.
   b. Carly could have already talked to her parents about her brother's disability and still want him to participate in activities like nondisabled kids.
   c. Other:

L: Look at the solutions again and choose one.

Which one would help you understand Alex the best?

V: Validate the solution by trying it.

Most students in the class will not have a sibling with a disability but can develop sensitivity to people with disabilities.

E: Evaluate how the solution worked.

This particular situation is not designed to "solve" the problem, but rather to help others understand the strengths of people with disabilities.

Extended Learning Activities

1. Problem-Solving Practice Scenario

Imagine you are asked to help coach people with disabilities in the Special Olympics, but you are not sure if you want to help out. How would you respond?

I: Identify the problem.

> ➤ You are asked to be a coach for the Special Olympics but are unsure if you want the job.

S: Solutions to the problem?

    a. Agree to participate as a coach.

    b. Politely say, "No, thank you."

    c. Other:

O: Obstacles to the solutions?

    a. There are not many obstacles to this solution other than it involves a time commitment.

    b. By not helping as a coach, you may be letting people down.

    c. Other:

L: Look at the solutions again and choose one.

Choose the solution that would help others as well as yourself.

V: Validate the solution by trying it.

Practice each possible solution as you role-play with your classmates.

E: Evaluate how the solution worked.

Remember that individuals with disabilities are just like everyone else. They enjoy laughing, playing, and being with people. Participating as a coach in the Special Olympics is a rewarding experience.

2. Reinforcement Activity

Give each student a copy of "Strength or Weakness." Tell students that each of us has different strengths and weaknesses. On the top half of the paper, students should write or draw (or both) about their strengths. On the bottom half of the paper, they should write or draw (or both) about their weaknesses. When all students are finished, allow time to share as well as locate classmates with similar strengths and weaknesses. Also, ask students to find someone whose strength is their weakness and vice versa.

Name:_____   Date: _____

Strength or Weakness

Directions: Each of us has different strengths and weaknesses. On the top half of the paper, write and/or draw about your strengths. On the bottom half of the paper, write and/or draw about your weaknesses.

My Strengths

My Weaknesses

Baby Duck and the Bad Eyeglasses

Title: *Baby Duck and the Bad Eyeglasses*
Author: Amy Hest
Copyright: 1996
Publisher: Candlewick Press
ISBN: 0-7636-0559-X
Topic: Vision difficulties
Approximate Grade Levels: K–2

Book Summary:

Baby Duck does not like the way she looks in her new eyeglasses. She does not think she can play or have fun with her glasses on. With the help of her grandpa, Baby Duck realizes glasses are okay.

Lesson Goal:

To help students recognize that glasses are a natural device many people wear.

Prereading Activities:

If you wear glasses, take them off and ask students if they notice anything different. Put the glasses back on and ask students if you look different. Tell students that even though we may look different when the glasses are on or off, we are still the same person inside. To show how important glasses are in general, an alternative for those not wearing glasses is to bring in clear plastic wrap. Cut a piece for each child and have them look through the plastic wrap at the board. What do they see? Children quickly learn how helpful glasses are.

During Reading:

Read the book aloud. Before revealing how Baby Duck solved the problem, stop and use the I SOLVE strategy to predict potential solutions. Use the discussion questions to check students' comprehension of the story.

Postreading/Discussion Questions:

1. What does it mean when the author writes that Baby Duck was "sizing up" her new glasses?

2. Why didn't she look like Baby Duck with the new glasses on?

3. Why wasn't Baby Duck excited to go to the park?

4. What does it mean when the Duck family "filed" out the front door?

5. Why don't Baby Duck's glasses have arms?

6. Why didn't Baby Duck dance down the lane?

7. Would you sing a sad song like Baby Duck? Why?

8. What did Grandpa do to cheer up Baby Duck?

9. Why did Baby Duck decide she could still run and splash?

10. Why were the letters on the new boat so clear?

I SOLVE Strategy

I: Identify the problem presented in the book.

➤ Baby Duck does not like the way she looks in her new eyeglasses.

S: Solutions to the problem?

a. Book solution: Baby Duck's grandpa pointed out the positive things about wearing glasses.

b. Baby Duck could have refused to wear her glasses.

c. Other:

O: Obstacles to the solutions?

a. Book solution: There might not always be a grandpa who can cheer up Baby Duck.

b. If Baby Duck refuses to wear the glasses, she will not see well.

c. Other:

L: Look at the solutions again and choose one.

Which solution could help Baby Duck feel good about wearing glasses?

V: Validate the solution by trying it.

Practice each possible solution as you role-play with your classmates.

E: Evaluate how the solution worked.

Did you feel better about wearing glasses? If the solution did not solve the problem, return to step **S** and see if any other solutions might work. Continue with the steps.

Extended Learning Activities

1. Problem-Solving Practice Scenario

Imagine you get a new haircut and you don't like the way you look. What could you do to solve the problem?

I: Identify the problem.

> ➤ You don't like the way your new haircut looks.

S: Solutions to the problem?

  a. Wear a hat.

  b. Say to yourself, "My haircut is fine. I won't worry about what other people say."

  c. Other:

O: Obstacles to the solutions?

  a. Wearing a hat is often prohibited in school.

  b. Thinking positive thoughts is a good solution, but it may be hard to ignore other kids' inappropriate comments.

  c. Other:

L: Look at the solutions again and choose one.

Choose the solution that would help you feel good about yourself.

V: Validate the solution by trying it.

Practice each possible solution as you role-play with your classmates.

E: Evaluate how the solution worked.

Did you get used to your new haircut? If it still bothers you, return to step **S** and consider another solution to try.

2. Reinforcement Activity

Give students a copy of the reinforcement activity "Goofy Glasses." Allow students to decorate the glasses. Students can try them on and look in a mirror. Ask students if they like their new look. Ask students if wearing glasses changed them as a person. Conclude by stating that how we look on the outside does not reveal anything about the type of person we are on the inside.

Goofy Glasses

Directions: Decorate the glasses and cut them out. Next, cut two holes for the eyes. Try the glasses on. Do you become a different person with glasses on? Write about why you do or do not become a different person by wearing glasses.

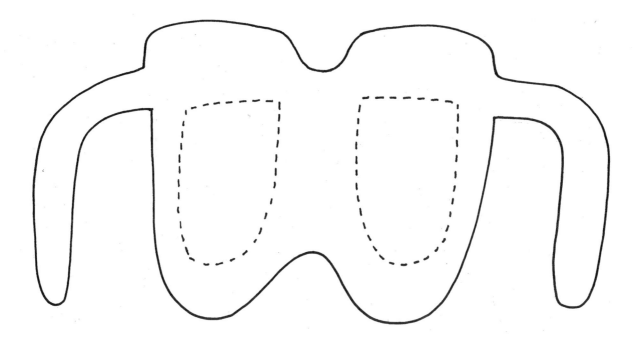

Do you "suddenly" become a different person when you wear glasses? Explain your answer on the lines below.

_____

_____

_____

_____

_____

Rolling Along: The Story of Taylor and His Wheelchair

Title: *Rolling Along: The Story of Taylor and His Wheelchair*
Author: Jamee Riggio Heelan
Copyright: 2000
Publisher: Peachtree
ISBN: 1-56145-219-X
Topic: Disability: Cerebral palsy
Approximate Grade Levels: K–3

Book Summary:

> Taylor is a young boy with cerebral palsy. His twin brother, Tyler, does not have cerebral palsy. The two brothers have more things in common than not. With the help of a wheelchair, Taylor can do as many things as his brother.

Lesson Goal:

> To help students understand cerebral palsy and the many abilities of individuals with disabilities.

Prereading Activities:

> Ask students if they know anyone who uses a wheelchair. It is likely that some students' grandparents are using a wheelchair. Explain that people in wheelchairs often have physical problems but may not have thinking problems. Show students the cover of the book and ask them to make predictions about the outcome.

During Reading:

> Read the book aloud. This story does not lend itself well to stopping and making predictions using the I SOLVE strategy. Discuss the story using the discussion questions if applicable.

Postreading/Discussion Questions:

1. What are some of the things Taylor and Tyler both enjoy?
2. What is cerebral palsy?
3. What is hard for Taylor to do?
4. Even though Taylor cannot walk, do you think he is still nice?
5. Would you be Taylor's friend? Why?
6. Why do some people use wheelchairs?
7. Why do some kids go to therapy?
8. Do you think it would be easy or hard to use a wheelchair?
9. How would Taylor feel if he was unable to get into a building in his wheelchair?
10. How is Taylor similar to you?

I SOLVE Strategy

I: Identify the problem presented in the book.

> ➤ Taylor has cerebral palsy and cannot walk by himself.

S: Solutions to the problem?

   a. Book solution: Attend therapy to get stronger, and rely on family and friends for assistance.

   b. Taylor tries to live as normal as possible, and he seems to maintain a positive attitude.

   c. Other:

O: Obstacles to the solutions?

   a–c: Obstacles will vary.

L: Look at the solutions again and choose one.

   When a person has cerebral palsy, there is no cure or magical solution. Students need to understand that people with cerebral palsy try to live life normally.

V: Validate the solution by trying it.

   The teacher may want to borrow a wheelchair and allow students to try maneuvering it throughout the school.

E: Evaluate how the solution worked.

   Is it hard to use a wheelchair? Why?

Extended Learning Activities

1. Problem-Solving Practice Scenario

> Imagine your leg is broken and you must use crutches. How would you carry your belongings from class to class? How can you solve this problem?

I: Identify the problem.

> ➤ You have a broken leg and cannot easily carry your belongings.

S: Solutions to the problem?

    a.   Ask a friend to carry your belongings.

    b.   Place your belongings in a backpack.

    c.   Other:

O: Obstacles to the solutions?

    a.   It may be difficult for a friend to always help you if he or she misses part of class.

    b.   The backpack may become too heavy to carry while on crutches.

    c.   Other:

L: Look at the solutions again and choose one.

Choose the solution that would solve the problem until your leg healed.

V: Validate the solution by trying it.

Practice each possible solution as you role-play with your classmates.

E: Evaluate how the solution worked.

If the solution worked, remember to use it if you ever break your leg. If the solution did not work, return to step **S**.

2.   Reinforcement Activity

Give each student a copy of the reinforcement activity "Four-Finger Challenge." Explain that you will use a piece of masking tape to gently secure each student's writing thumb to the palm of his or her hand. Now ask students to pick up a pencil and write their name, address, and telephone number on the piece of paper. Notice the responses from students as they attempt this challenge. Students will either not be able to write or write sloppily. Explain that individuals with a disability must learn ways to overcome or compensate for their disability. Ask students how they compensated for not being able to use their thumb to write. List the ideas on the board and allow students to try some of the suggestions.

Name:_____   Date: _____

Four-Finger Challenge

Directions: After your teacher gently tapes the thumb of your writing hand to your palm, try to write your name, address, and phone number on the lines below. Why was this difficult? How were you able to write differently?

Name: _____

Street address: _____

City: _____

State: _____

Zip code: _____

Telephone number: _____

Additional Readings on Disabilities

Title and Author: *Glasses: Who Needs 'Em?* by Lanae Smith
ISBN: 0-670-84160-9
Approximate Grade Levels: K–3
Copyright: 1991

Book Summary:
> This book describes the zany adventure of a young boy as he visits the optometrist for an eye exam and glasses.

Title and Author: *We'll Paint the Octopus Red* by Stephanie Stuve-Bodeen
ISBN: 1-890627-06-2
Approximate Grade Levels: K–3
Copyright: 1998

Book Summary:
> A young girl is excited about all the things she can do with her new brother or sister. One day Dad tells her the baby is born with Down's syndrome. Together the two realize that with help and extra patience, the sister can still do all the things she planned with the baby.

Title and Author: *I Have a Sister, My Sister Is Deaf* by Jeanne Whitehouse Peterson
ISBN: 0-06-024702-9
Approximate Grade Levels: K–3
Copyright: 1977

Book Summary:
> A young girl shares her perspective living with a younger sister who is deaf. This book helps explain deafness in terms kids will easily understand and relate to.

Helping Students Value Diversity

Schools comprise people with diverse backgrounds. Although there is diversity among people, students do not often recognize that people frequently have more similarities than differences. Each lesson plan in this chapter helps students learn to respect human differences and positively relate to others.

Uncle Jed's Barbershop

Title: *Uncle Jed's Barbershop*
Author: Margaree King Mitchell
Copyright: 1993
Publisher: Aladdin Paperbacks
ISBN: 0-689-81913-7
Topic: Diversity
Approximate Grade Levels: K–3

Book Summary:

Uncle Jed is a barber who always dreams of having his own barbershop. He travels throughout several counties cutting people's hair and saving his money. He faces many obstacles, such as the Great Depression, but with hard work and faith in his dream, Uncle Jed achieves his goal.

Lesson Goal:

To help students value human diversity and positively relate to others.

Prereading Activities:

Tell students that today's book is about a barber. Ask students if they know what a barber does for a living. Tell them this book takes place in the early 1900s when things were much different from how they are now. Tell students to listen and see if they can identify some things that were different from how they are today.

During Reading:

Read the book aloud. Before revealing whether Uncle Jed saved enough money to open his barbershop, stop and use the I SOLVE strategy to predict potential ideas for Uncle Jed to save or earn money. Discuss the story using the discussion questions if applicable.

Postreading/Discussion Questions:

1. How old do you think the little girl, Sara Jean, is when this story begins?

2. Why wouldn't Sara Jean's mother allow Uncle Jed to cut her hair?

3. What is Uncle Jed's dream?

4. Why didn't people believe Uncle Jed could save enough money for his shop?

5. What does the word *segregation* mean?

6. How do you think Sara Jean's parents felt when they had to wait for the doctor to treat all the white patients first?

7. How did it make Uncle Jed feel to help Sara Jean get the operation?

8. How do you think Uncle Jed felt when he heard the bank lost all his money?

9. Why did Uncle Jed keep trying to open a barbershop when he was having so many troubles?

10. What do you think Sara Jean dreamed?

I SOLVE Strategy

I: Identify the problem presented in the book.

➤ Uncle Jed did not have enough money to open his own barbershop.

S: Solutions to the problem?

a. Book solution: Uncle Jed continued to believe in himself and work toward achieving his goal of owning a barbershop.

b. Uncle Jed could have given up on his dream and settled for being a traveling barber.

c. Other:

O: Obstacles to the solutions?

    a. Book solution: Uncle Jed had many obstacles to overcome, such as losing his savings when the banks closed. Some people would have given up, but Uncle Jed continued to work hard toward reaching his dream.

    b. If Uncle Jed gave up, he never would have achieved the kind of success he wanted.

    c. Other:

L: Look at the solutions again and choose one.

Which one could help Uncle Jed maintain his focus and achieve his goal?

V: Validate the solution by trying it.

Practice each possible solution as you role-play with your classmates.

E: Evaluate how the solution worked.

How do you think your solution worked? If the solution did not solve the problem, return to step **S** and see if any other solutions might work. Continue with the steps.

Extended Learning Activities

1. Problem-Solving Practice Scenario

> While playing with your friends, you tell them that you want to be an athlete in the Olympics when you get older. Your friends laugh and say, "Yeah, right!" What would you do and say?

I: Identify the problem.

    ➤ Your friends do not believe you can achieve your dream of participating in the Olympics.

S: Solutions to the problem?

    a. Say, "You're probably right. It is so hard to make it to the Olympics."

    b. Practice harder so that you will continue to improve and work toward your dream.

    c. Other:

O: Obstacles to the solutions?

    a.   Putting yourself down is no way to reach your dream.

    b.   Practicing may or may not help you improve, but you will know you tried your hardest.

    c.   Other:

L: Look at the solutions again and choose one.

Choose the solution that would show your friends your seriousness about taking small steps toward your dream.

V: Validate the solution by trying it.

Achieving your dream takes time, but continuous progress helps increase your chances for success. Role-play each possible solution.

E: Evaluate how the solution worked.

How did your friends react to your response? Revisit the other solutions and try again if needed.

2. Reinforcement Activity

Give each student a copy of "My Dream—My Goal." Tell students it is important for everyone to have a dream or goal they want to achieve. To achieve that goal, students must clearly focus on and work each day toward their goal. Tell students to write about or draw a picture of their goal as well as list at least one thing they can do today to begin achieving their goal.

Name:_____ Date: _____

My Dream—My Goal

Directions: Uncle Jed's goal was to own a barbershop. Think about something you want to achieve or be when you get older. Write and/or draw a picture about your goal. Write down at least one thing you can do to work toward the goal.

Angel Child, Dragon Child

Title: *Angel Child, Dragon Child*
Author: Michele Maria Surat
Copyright: 1989
Publisher: Scholastic
ISBN: 0-590-42271-5
Topic: Diversity
Approximate Grade Levels: K–3

Book Summary:

Ut is Vietnamese, and her family just arrived in the United States without her mother. The children in school make fun of the way she talks and dresses. Raymond picks on her almost every day, but surprisingly he ends up helping her raise money for her mother's trip to the United States.

Lesson Goal:

To help students recognize all people have feelings and that we should not judge people by their dialect or customs.

Prereading Activities:

Show students the book cover and ask them to make predictions about the story. Write the predictions on the board. Tell students that the story is about a girl who just started school after coming to America from Vietnam.

During Reading:

Read the book aloud. Before revealing how Ut solved her problem, stop and use the I SOLVE strategy to predict potential solutions. Discuss the story using the discussion questions if applicable.

Postreading/Discussion Questions:

1. Why did the other children say that Ut was wearing pajamas?

2. How did Ut feel when the teacher asked her to write her name?

3. What did Ut mean when she hid her "dragon face"?

4. Who does Ut live with?

5. What did the boy hit Ut with?

6. Why didn't Ut want to be an Angel Child for Raymond?

7. Why was Raymond crying?

8. What did Raymond learn by writing Ut's story?

9. How will the children earn money for Ut's mother?

10. How did Ut like school after the other students understood her story? Why?

I SOLVE Strategy

I: Identify the problem presented in the book.

➤ Ut is not accepted by the other students in school because she dresses and talks differently.

S: Solutions to the problem?

   a. Book solution: Ut told Raymond her story after the two of them got in trouble with the school principal. When the principal read Ut's story to the class, the students understood and accepted her.

   b. Ut could have become so lonely that she stopped coming to school.

   c. Other:

O: Obstacles to the solutions?

   a. Book solution: Once the children understood Ut's story, they raised money to bring her mother to America.

   b. If Ut stopped coming to school, she would fail her subjects.

   c. Other:

L: Look at the solutions again and choose one.

Which solution could help you if others did not understand your customs?

V: Validate the solution by trying it.

Practice each possible solution as you role-play with your classmates.

E: Evaluate how the solution worked.

Remember to choose a solution that will help others understand your customs as well as solve the problem. If the solution did not solve the problem, return to step **S** and see if any other solutions might work. Continue with the steps.

Extended Learning Activities

1. Problem-Solving Practice Scenario

Imagine it is your birthday. Instead of having a cake to celebrate, you have sliced tomatoes. The other kids laugh at you and think you are weird. How would you respond?

I: Identify the problem.

➤ The kids do not understand your customs and laugh at you.

S: Solutions to the problem?

    a. Tell the other kids they are weird for not eating healthy foods.

    b. Explain that your family has different traditions, and this is the food you use to celebrate birthdays.

    c. Other:

O: Obstacles to the solutions?

    a. Teasing the other kids does not solve the problem.

    b. Some kids still may tease you even if you explain your family traditions.

    c. Other:

L: Look at the solutions again and choose one.

Choose the solution that would solve the problem in the long run.

V: Validate the solution by trying it.

Practice each possible solution as you role-play with your classmates.

E: Evaluate how the solution worked.

Did you find a solution you think would solve the problem? If not, return to step **S** and try again.

2. Reinforcement Activity

Give each student a copy of "My Story." Tell students that each person has a story or family history. Sometimes we do not understand where others are from or what they are like outside of school. Ask students to create a timeline of their personal history. Students can begin from when they were born until the present. Use pictures or words to tell the story.

My Story

Directions: Each person has a story or family history. Create a timeline of your personal history from when you were born until the present. Use pictures or words to tell the story.

The Black Snowman

Title: *The Black Snowman*
Author: Phil Mendez
Copyright: 1989
Publisher: Scholastic
ISBN: 0-590-44873-0
Topic: Diversity
Approximate Grade Levels: 1–3

Book Summary:

Jacob and his brother live in the inner city and find a *kente*, an African storytelling shawl. The boys think it is a scrap of cloth, but they soon realize it has magical qualities when they put it on a snowman and later encounter a fire.

Lesson Goal:

To help students understand that happiness does not come from having lots of money or being part of a particular ethnic group but rather from believing in oneself and one's heritage.

Prereading Activities:

Ask students if they know the story of Frosty the Snowman. Choose one student to tell the story. Ask students if they know any other stories about snowmen. Tell students there is an African folktale about a very different snowman. Show them the book's cover and ask students to make predictions about the story.

During Reading:

Read the book aloud. Before revealing how Peewee is saved from the fire, stop and use the I SOLVE strategy to predict potential solutions. Discuss the story using the discussion questions if applicable.

Postreading/Discussion Questions:

1. What do you learn about Jacob from the way the author describes his lamp?
2. Why does Jacob's mother yell at him?
3. Why doesn't Jacob like being black?
4. What made the *kente* magic?
5. How did the boys feel when the snowman began to speak?
6. What did the snowman mean when he said, "Have you sat at the table of your forefathers"?
7. Was Jacob dreaming when he heard the snowman calling him?
8. What do you think will happen to Peewee when he leaves the apartment?
9. How did Jacob feel when the snowman melted?
10. What did Jacob learn from this experience?

I SOLVE Strategy

I: Identify the problem presented in the book.

➤ Jacob does not like his color because he does not understand his heritage.

S: Solutions to the problem?

    a. Book solution: Jacob learns about his heritage when his brother and he find a *kente*, a shawl with magical powers, and place it on a snowman.

    b. Jacob could have asked his mother to tell him stories about their family history.

    c. Other:

O: Obstacles to the solutions?

    a. Book solution: Students must understand that this story is an African folktale and that finding a magical *kente* today is only a make-believe solution.

    b. Jacob may not have understood how to ask his mother about their family history; this is a skill that develops with maturity.

    c. Other:

L: Look at the solutions again and choose one.

Which one would help you learn about your heritage?

V: Validate the solution by trying it.

Discuss each possible solution with your classmates.

E: Evaluate how the solution worked.

Remember that understanding our past helps us in the future.

Extended Learning Activities

1. Problem-Solving Practice Scenario

Imagine you want to buy a new purse for your mother's birthday, but you don't have enough money. How could you solve this problem?

I: Identify the problem.

➤ You do not have enough money to purchase a new purse for your mother's birthday.

S: Solutions to the problem?

    a.   Instead of the purse, make a craft for your mother.

    b.   Ask an adult to help you pay for the purse.

    c.   Other:

O: Obstacles to the solutions?

    a.   You may not have the necessary materials to make the craft.

    b.   The adult you ask may not give you money to buy the purse.

    c.   Other:

L: Look at the solutions again and choose one.

Choose the solution that would show your mother you cared about her.

V: Validate the solution by trying it.

Discuss each possible solution as you role-play with your classmates.

E: Evaluate how the solution worked.

Did you decide on a solution that shows your mother you care for her? If you do not think the first solution you selected will work, return to step **S** and choose another solution.

2. Reinforcement Activity

Give each student a copy of "*Kente.*" Remind students that the *kente*'s magical powers brought the snowman to life and helped save Peewee during the fire. Ask students to imagine they found a *kente* while playing. How would they use the magical powers of the *kente*? Have students write or draw a story about their adventure.

Name:_____   Date:_____

Kente

Directions: Imagine you found a *kente* while playing. How would you use the magical powers of the *kente*? Write and/or draw a story about how you would use the *kente*.

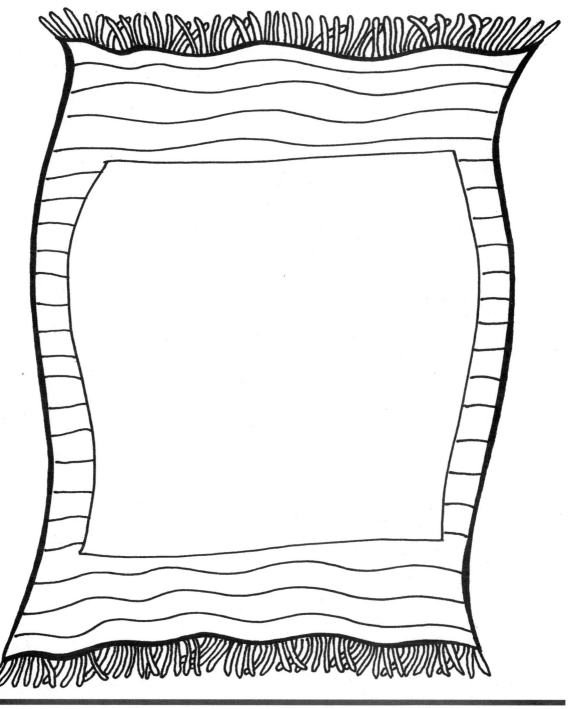

Wings

Title: *Wings*
Author: Christopher Myers
Copyright: 2000
Publisher: Scholastic
ISBN: 0-590-03377-8
Topic: Diversity
Approximate Grade Levels: 1–3

Book Summary:

Ikarus, a new boy in school, is made fun of because he has wings and is different from the other kids. Another student, who also is made fun of because she is shy, sticks up for Ikarus, and together they find strength in one another.

Lesson Goal:

To help students recognize that being different is not bad; each person has different strengths, and the world needs people of differing abilities.

Prereading Activities:

Ask students to first raise their hands if they think it would be great to have wings and then raise their hands if it would be bad to have wings. Tell students to imagine they have wings. What are some of the things they could do with wings? Tell students that today's book is about a boy with wings; however, in this book the boy is made fun of because he has wings.

During Reading:

Read the book aloud. Before revealing how Ikarus is accepted, stop and use the I SOLVE strategy to predict potential solutions. Discuss the story using the discussion questions if applicable.

Postreading/Discussion Questions:

1. Why doesn't the book's narrator think Ikarus is strange?

2. Does the narrator like it when other students whisper about her?

3. Why did the teacher complain about Ikarus's wings?

4. How did Ikarus feel when he left the classroom?

5. Do you think if Ikarus flies, the other kids will stop laughing at him?

6. Why weren't the other kids impressed with Ikarus's flying?

7. What could the narrator have said to the mean kids as they made fun of Ikarus?

8. Could the policeman put Ikarus in jail for being too different?

9. Why did the narrator girl speak up for Ikarus?

10. How did the narrator and Ikarus feel at the end of the story? Why?

I SOLVE Strategy

I: Identify the problem presented in the book.

> ➤ Students make fun of Ikarus because he looks different and the narrator because she is shy.

S: Solutions to the problem?

    a. Book solution: When the story narrator sees other kids picking on Ikarus, she finds the courage to speak up for and defend Ikarus.

    b. The narrator could have decided not to speak up and waited to talk to Ikarus in private.

    c. Other:

O: Obstacles to the solutions?

    a. Book solution: Sometimes people will not stand up for other people if they do not know them well.

    b. Often there is no perfect time to talk in private.

    c. Other:

L: Look at the solutions again and choose one.

Which one could help you stand up for yourself if kids were making fun of you?

V: Validate the solution by trying it.

Practice each possible solution as you role-play with your classmates.

E: Evaluate how the solution worked.

Remember to choose a solution that will help you feel good about yourself as well as solve the problem. If the solution did not solve the problem, return to step **S** and see if any other solutions might work. Continue with the steps.

Extended Learning Activities

1. Problem-Solving Practice Scenario

Imagine your older brother or sister eats the last piece of cake when they knew it was saved for you. What would you do?

I: Identify the problem.

  ➤ Your brother or sister ate your last piece of cake.

S: Solutions to the problem?

  a. Demand they buy you a new cake.

  b. Tell your mother.

  c. Other:

O: Obstacles to the solutions?

  a. Your brother or sister may laugh at you when you demand a new cake.

  b. Your mother may scold your sibling, but it will not make the cake reappear.

  c. Other:

L: Look at the solutions again and choose one.

  Choose the solution that would peacefully solve the problem.

V: Validate the solution by trying it.

  Practice each possible solution as you role-play with your classmates.

E: Evaluate how the solution worked.

  What did you learn from this role play? Which solution could work best for you?

2. Reinforcement Activity

Give each student a copy of "Same Old, Same Old." Tell students to imagine every person in the world dressed, talked, walked, and acted the same way. Explain that furthermore, everyone is interested in the same music and sports and has the same interests and tastes. Ask students to write a story about what the world would be like if everyone were the same. Students can also write about why it is positive that everyone is different.

Same Old, Same Old

Directions: Imagine every person in the world dressed, talked, walked, and acted the same way. Also, everyone is interested in the same music, sports, and has the same interests and tastes. Write a story about what it would be like to live in a world like this. What would the good and bad things be?

The Hundred Dresses

Title: *The Hundred Dresses*
Author: Eleanor Estes
Copyright: 1972
Publisher: Harcourt
ISBN: 0-15-642350-2
Topic: Diversity
Approximate Grade Levels: 2–3 (This is a chapter book.)

Book Summary:

Wanda wears the same dress every day, even though she tells the girls in her class that she has 100 dresses lined up in her closet at home. Two of the girls start to tease her about the dresses as well as her last name. One girl feels remorseful but does not have the courage to stand up for Wanda.

Lesson Goal:

To help students learn that we must stand up for our own beliefs even if our friends do not agree.

Prereading Activities:

Show students the cover of the book and ask them to predict the content. Ask students if anyone can have 100 dresses. Explain that the main character in the book claims to have 100 dresses, even though she is very poor.

During Reading:

Read the book aloud. Before revealing the father's letter about the move, stop and use the I SOLVE strategy to predict potential solutions. Discuss the story using the discussion questions if applicable.

Postreading/Discussion Questions:

Chapter 1—Were Peggy and Maddie friends with Wanda?

Chapter 2—What kind of fun did the girls have with Wanda?

Chapter 3—How did the dresses game begin? Do you think Wanda had 100 dresses in her closet?

Chapter 4—Why won't Maddie stand up to Peggy and tell her to stop asking Wanda how many dresses she has? What were the boys and girls to draw for the contest?

Chapter 5—How does Maddie feel after hearing the letter from Wanda's father? Why? Why did the girls want to go and find Wanda after school let out?

Chapter 6—Are the girls right to think their teasing made Wanda move away? Why did Maddie decide that she was never going to stand by and let someone get picked on?

Chapter 7—What did Peggy and Maddie learn from this experience with Wanda?

I SOLVE Strategy

I: Identify the problem presented in the book.

> ➤ Wanda is made fun of because she wears the same dress every day and tells the girls in her class she has 100 dresses.

S: Solutions to the problem?

    a. Book solution: Wanda moves away, and the girls feel bad that they made fun of her.

    b. Maddie could have stood up to Peggy and told her to stop asking Wanda about the 100 dresses.

    c. Other:

O: Obstacles to the solutions?

    a. Book solution: It may be very difficult to move away when faced with a problem.

    b. Maddie did not have enough courage to stand up for what she believed.

    c. Other:

L: Look at the solutions again and choose one.

Which solution would solve this problem?

V: Validate the solution by trying it.

Practice each possible solution as you role-play with your classmates.

E: Evaluate how the solution worked.

Did the solution seem to solve the problem in the long term? If the solution did not solve the problem, return to step **S** and see if any other solutions might work. Continue with the steps.

Extended Learning Activities

1. Problem-Solving Practice Scenario

Imagine it is lunchtime in school, and you and another student have identical lunch boxes. When you open your lunch, it is the wrong one. As you walk over to the person, you see that your classmate is already eating your lunch! What would you do or say to solve this problem?

I: Identify the problem.

> ➤ A classmate is eating the wrong lunch—your lunch.

S: Solutions to the problem?

    a.   Begin yelling at the classmate for eating part of your lunch.

    b.   Tell the classmate that today you'll switch lunches and just eat the other lunch instead of your own.

    c.   Other:

O: Obstacles to the solutions?

    a.   Yelling at the classmate might upset both of you.

    b.   You may not want to eat the classmate's lunch if you do not like the food.

    c.   Other:

L: Look at the solutions again and choose one.

Choose the solution that would calmly solve the problem and help you get your lunch back.

V: Validate the solution by trying it.

Practice each possible solution as you role-play with your classmates.

E: Evaluate how the solution worked.

Which solution seemed the best for handling this problem? If you did not find a solution to effectively solve the problem, return to step **S** and reevaluate the remaining solutions.

2. Reinforcement Activity

Give each student a copy of "Stand Up." Tell students that it is important to stand up for the values we believe. Ask students to begin by drawing a picture of a dress or motorboat. Next, students should write about what they would do or say if a student in the class said she had 100 dresses at home.

Stand Up

Directions: In the space below, draw a dress or a motorboat.

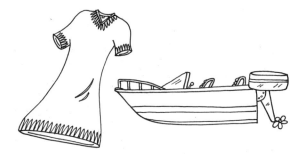

What would you do or say if a classmate said she had 100 dresses at home? Would you make fun of the student? Explain your answer on the lines below.

_____

_____

_____

_____

Additional Readings on Diversity

Title and Author: *Dancing in the Wings* by Debbie Allen
ISBN: 0-803-72501-9
Approximate Grade Levels: K–3
Copyright: 2000

Book Summary:
> This book is about a ballerina who is made fun of because she is taller than the rest of the ballet students. The book teaches children to not let what people say discourage them from achieving their dreams.

Title and Author: *The Crayon Box That Talked* by Shane Derolf
ISBN: 0-679-88611-7
Approximate Grade Levels: K–3
Copyright: 1997

Book Summary:
> This book is about a box of crayons that do not get along until a young girl with a positive outlook uses them to draw a picture. The crayons realize that the uniqueness of each crayon contributes to creating a beautiful picture.

Title and Author: *The Name Jar* by Yangsook Choi
ISBN: 0-375-80613-X
Approximate Grade Levels: K–3
Copyright: 2001

Book Summary:
> Yoon-hye is teased about her name on the school bus, so she decides to choose an American name. Her classmates fill a jar with suggested names for Yoon-hye, but with the help of a classmate, she decides to keep her own name.

Helping Students Learn About Sharing and Selfishness

Sharing is a difficult concept for children to learn. Each lesson in this chapter helps teach children manners for appropriately sharing and teaches children that only thinking about ourselves and not others makes it difficult to attain friends.

It's Mine!

Title: *It's Mine!*
Author: Leo Lionni
Copyright: 1996
Publisher: Dragonfly Books
ISBN: 0-394-97000-4
Topic: Sharing
Approximate Grade Levels: K–3

Book Summary:

Three young frogs are continually bickering over who owns each part of the island they live on. One day a large toad, who hears the bickering from the other side of the island, tells the frogs that the bickering is unpleasant. During a strong storm, the frogs learn the importance of sharing.

Lesson Goal:

To help students understand the benefits of sharing.

Prereading Activities:

Ask students to name some things they share with friends during school. Write these on the board. Next ask students to think about what the class would be like if no one shared. Conclude by saying, "If no one shared, there would be lots of arguing." Show students the book cover and ask them to predict what the frogs in the story are arguing about.

During Reading:

Read the book aloud. Before reading the part about the water receding, stop and use the I SOLVE strategy to predict potential solutions. Discuss the story using the discussion questions if applicable.

Postreading/Discussion Questions:

1.   Where does this story take place?

2.   What does the word *quarrelsome* mean?

3.   Why did the frogs quarrel?

4.   What did the toad say to the frogs?

5.   Why didn't the toad tell the frogs to stop bickering?

6.   Did the frogs listen to the toad?

7.   Why were the frogs scared?

8.   What made the frogs feel better even though they were cold and scared?

9.   Why did the toad save the frogs?

10.   Why did the frogs feel happy in a way they never had before?

I SOLVE Strategy

I: Identify the problem presented in the book.

➤ The three frogs quarreled all the time.

S: Solutions to the problem?

a.   Book solution: The frogs had to rely on each other to survive the storm and realized they could share.

b.   The three frogs could have asked the toad for advice on how to stop quarreling.

c.   Other:

O: Obstacles to the solutions?

a.   Book solution: The frogs were fortunate there was a storm that helped bring them closer together.

b.   Perhaps the toad would not have agreed to help the frogs learn to stop quarreling.

c.   Other:

L: Look at the solutions again and choose one.

Which solution could have helped the frogs learn to share?

V: Validate the solution by trying it.

Practice each possible solution as you role-play with your classmates.

E: Evaluate how the solution worked.

Remember to choose a solution that helps everyone learn to share. If the solution did not solve the problem, return to step **S** and see if any other solutions might work. Continue with the remaining steps.

Extended Learning Activities

1. Problem-Solving Practice Scenario

Imagine you ride your bicycle to the neighborhood park. Upon arriving, you always like to play with the toys in the sandbox. A child already playing in the sandbox says, "You can't play with these toys—they are all mine!" What would you do or say?

I: Identify the problem.

➤ A child in the sandbox does not want to share the toys.

S: Solutions to the problem?

    a. Tell the other child that the toys belong to everyone, and grab some out of the child's hands.

    b. Walk away and hope the child leaves soon so you can go and play in the sandbox.

    c. Other:

O: Obstacles to the solutions?

    a. Telling the child that the toys belong to everyone is a good idea, but grabbing some of the toys away from the child does not peacefully solve the problem.

    b. If you walk away, you do not feel satisfied, because the other child is still playing with the toys and not sharing.

    c. Other:

L: Look at the solutions again and choose one.

Choose the solution that would help show the child how to share.

V: Validate the solution by trying it.

Practice each possible solution as you role-play with your classmates.

E: Evaluate how the solution worked.

If you think the child would share after you use your solution, way to go! If you think the solution is unsuccessful, then return to step **S** and review the remaining solutions.

2. Reinforcement Activity

Give each student a copy of "Mine and Yours." Tell students that most of the time, sharing with others is the best solution for solving problems. But sometimes we have special items that we do not have to share. Ask students to list in the first column all of the items they will share and in the second column the things they do not like to share. For example, students may write that they will share their scooter but will not share their toothbrush.

Name:_____   Date: _____

Mine and Yours

Directions: In column one, list all the things that you share with friends. In column two, list all the things that you would not share with friends.

Column One: Things I'd Share	Column Two: Things I Would NOT Share
Example: Some of my potato chips.	***Example***: My toothbrush.

Ebb and Flo and the Greedy Gulls

Title: *Ebb and Flo and the Greedy Gulls*
Author: Jane Simmons
Copyright: 1999
Publisher: Margaret K. McElderry
ISBN: 0-689-82484-X
Topic: Sharing
Approximate Grade Levels: K–3

Book Summary:

Ebb and Flo are at the beach for a picnic. When Ebb falls asleep, seagulls eat all the sandwiches. Flo accuses Ebb of eating all the sandwiches. Ebb's feeling are hurt, so he goes off by himself until Flo realizes that the seagulls ate the sandwiches.

Lesson Goal:

To teach students that falsely accusing someone before understanding the situation is unfair.

Prereading Activities:

Ask students if they have ever been accused of something they did not do. Show students the book's cover and explain that the same thing happens in this story. Tell students to listen carefully as you read the story aloud.

During Reading:

Read the book aloud. Before revealing how Flo determined the seagulls ate the food, stop and use the I SOLVE strategy to predict potential solutions. Discuss the story using the discussion questions if applicable.

Postreading/Discussion Questions:

1. Where does this story take place?

2. Why did the mom put out all of the food?

3. What happened while Ebb was snoozing?

4. How did Ebb feel when Flo accused him of eating all the sandwiches?

5. Why did the seagulls laugh?

6. What does the word *sulked* mean?

7. Why did Ebb feel that things were unfair?

8. How did Mom find out Ebb did not eat all the sandwiches?

9. Why didn't anyone help Ebb when the boat drifted out to sea?

10. How did Flo feel when she said, "I'm sorry I blamed you"?

I SOLVE Strategy

I: Identify the problem presented in the book.

> ➤ Flo thinks Ebb ate all the sandwiches.

S: Solutions to the problem?

    a. Book solution: While packing up during the rainstorm, Flo saw the seagulls eating their other food out of the picnic basket.

    b. Flo could have said, "It's no big deal, Ebb, we have other food to eat."

    c. Other:

O: Obstacles to the solutions?

    a. Book solution: If Ebb and Flo finished eating all the food, Flo would not have seen the seagulls eating from the picnic basket.

    b. If Flo just said, "It's okay, Ebb, we have other food to eat," then she would never have learned the seagulls ate the sandwiches and would have always blamed Ebb.

    c. Other:

L: Look at the solutions again and choose one.

Which one could help you solve the problem if someone ate your food?

V: Validate the solution by trying it.

Practice each possible solution as you role-play with your classmates.

E: Evaluate how the solution worked.

Remember to choose a solution that will help solve the problem and help you to learn all the facts of the situation. If the solution did not solve the problem, return to step **S** and see if any other solutions might work. Continue with the steps.

Extended Learning Activities

1. Problem-Solving Practice Scenario

Imagine a person in your class goes into your desk without your permission and takes one of your pencils. What would you do?

I: Identify the problem.

> ➤ A pencil is missing from your desk. You suspect that another student took it.

S: Solutions to the problem?

    a.   Tell an adult.

    b.   Look around the classroom and see if anyone is writing with your pencil.

    c.   Other:

O: Obstacles to the solutions?

    a.   Telling an adult may be the best solution in a situation like this.

    b.   You may not see anyone using your pencil even though it is missing from your desk.

    c.   Other:

L: Look at the solutions again and choose one.

Choose the solution that would solve the problem in the long run.

V: Validate the solution by trying it.

Practice each possible solution as you role-play with your classmates.

E: Evaluate how the solution worked.

Which solution helped to solve the problem?

2. Reinforcement Activity

Give each student a copy of the reinforcement activity "An Interview with Ebb." Tell students to imagine they are Ebb and put themselves in his place. Imagine they were on the beach snoozing and woke up to find the sandwiches were missing. Tell students to pretend the local newspaper wants to write a story about the event. In pairs, students will work to interview each other. Students take turns playing the role of the reporter and the role of Ebb. The reporter can ask Ebb questions and then write down his answers. After playing both parts, each person can write a newspaper story about Ebb.

Name:_____   Date: _____

An Interview with Ebb

Directions: This activity requires you to work with a partner. Each of you will take turns playing the roles of Ebb and a reporter. The reporter interviews Ebb by asking the questions listed below and writing Ebb's answers. When both people have finished a turn as Ebb and as a reporter, write a newspaper article about what happened.

Interview Questions:

1. What was the weather like at the beach?

2. Why did you decide to take a nap instead of exploring?

3. How did the seagulls wake you up?

4. What did you think when you saw the sandwiches were gone?

5. How did you feel when Flo and Mom said you ate the sandwiches?

6. Was it scary being out in the boat alone?

7. What did you do when Flo said, "I love you"?

8. Other:

Write your newspaper story on the lines or on another piece of paper.

_____

_____

_____   _____

Mean Soup

Title: *Mean Soup*
Author: Betsy Everitt
Copyright: 1992
Publisher: Harcourt, Brace
ISBN: 0-15-253146-7
Topic: Sharing
Approximate Grade Levels: K–2

Book Summary:

Horace has a horrible day at school, so when he gets home, his mother helps him make a pot of mean soup, and together they stir away his bad day.

Lesson Goal:

To help students recognize that sharing our feelings helps make us feel better.

Prereading Activities:

Show students the book's cover and ask them if they have ever felt mean. Ask students if they ever shared their mean feelings to make them go away. Explain that sharing our emotions can help us feel better.

During Reading:

Read the book aloud. Before revealing that Horace's mother is going to make mean soup, stop and use the I SOLVE strategy to predict potential solutions. Discuss the story using the discussion questions if applicable.

Postreading/Discussion Questions:

1. How old is Horace?

2. Why didn't Horace like Zelda's note?

3. How would Horace feel if the cow stepped on his foot?

4. Who is Mrs. Pearl?

5. What did Horace do when his mother said, "Hello"?

6. Why wasn't Horace saying much to his mother?

7. Did Horace want to make soup? Why?

8. How do you think Horace reacted when his mother screamed into the pot of water?

9. Why did making soup help Horace feel better?

10. How did you know Horace felt better?

I SOLVE Strategy

I: Identify the problem presented in the book.

> ➤ Horace has a horrible day and he feels mean.

S: Solutions to the problem?

    a. Book solution: Horace's mother helps him make mean soup to share his angry feelings.

    b. Horace could have drawn a picture about his mean feelings.

    c. Other:

O: Obstacles to the solutions?

    a. Book solution: Sometimes when feeling mean, there might not be a place around to make mean soup.

    b. Horace may not like to draw.

    c. Other:

L: Look at the solutions again and choose one.

Which solution could help you share your mean feelings?

V: Validate the solution by trying it.

Practice each possible solution as you role-play with your classmates.

E: Evaluate how the solution worked.

Remember to choose a solution that will help you share your feelings in a good way. If the solution did not solve the problem, return to step **S** and see if any other solutions might work. Continue with the steps.

Extended Learning Activities

1. Problem-Solving Practice Scenario

Imagine you borrowed a book from the school library and now you cannot find it. What should you do?

I: Identify the problem.

➤ You cannot find your library book.

S: Solutions to the problem?

    a. Tell the librarian you cannot find the book and see what the librarian says.

    b. Go on a thorough search and look everywhere you can think of to try and find the book.

    c. Other:

O: Obstacles to the solutions?

    a. The librarian may not allow you to check out another book if you do not turn in your current book.

    b. You may not find the missing book even after a thorough search.

    c. Other:

L: Look at the solutions again and choose one.

Choose the solution that would solve the problem and prevent it from occurring again.

V: Validate the solution by trying it.

Practice each possible solution as you role-play with your classmates.

E: Evaluate how the solution worked.

Which solution seems best for keeping track of the library book?

2. Reinforcement Activity

Give each student a copy of "Mean Soup." Tell students to think about the ingredients Horace put into his mean soup: a scream, a growl, a stuck-out tongue, a bang, and dragon breath. Students should think about and then write the ingredients they would put into their mean soup the next time they feel mean.

Mean Soup

Directions: Think about the ingredients Horace put into his mean soup: a scream, a growl, a stuck-out tongue, a bang, and dragon breath. If you felt mean, think about and then write the ingredients you would put into your mean soup.

Franklin Is Bossy

Title: *Franklin Is Bossy*
Author: Paulette Bourgeois
Copyright: 1997
Publisher: Kids Can Press
ISBN: 1-55074-119-5
Topic: Sharing
Approximate Grade Levels: K–3

Book Summary:

Franklin decides all the games to play with his friends and does not listen to their ideas. Franklin's friends decide not to play with him anymore until he learns to share the decision making.

Lesson Goal:

To help students recognize that if they do not share with others, they will not have many friends.

Prereading Activities:

Ask students what it means to be bossy. Summarize by telling students they will not make many friends if they do not share with others. Ask them to predict what Franklin does in the story.

During Reading:

Read the book aloud. Before revealing how Franklin solves the problem, stop and use the I SOLVE strategy to predict potential solutions. Discuss the story using the discussion questions if applicable.

Postreading/Discussion Questions:

1. Why did Franklin want to always pick the games?

2. How did Franklin's friends feel when he changed the game rules at the end of the game?

3. How did Franklin act that tells the reader he is upset?

4. What did Franklin do in his room?

5. Were Franklin's friends having fun without him? Why?

6. What did Franklin say that was bossy?

7. How did Franklin decide it was best to apologize to Bear?

8. How did Franklin feel when his friends all shouted, "No fair, Franklin"?

9. How did Franklin react when his friends said he had to play in the outfield?

10. Did Franklin play as a team member?

I SOLVE Strategy

I: Identify the problem presented in the book.

> ➤ Franklin is bossy and does not share any decisions with his friends.

S: Solutions to the problem?

    a. Book solution: Franklin heard his father and Owl talking about how they apologized to solve their argument.

    b. Franklin could have asked his friends for ideas.

    c. Other:

O: Obstacles to the solutions?

    a. Book solution: Apologizing is always a good idea.

    b. Franklin may have been too shy or afraid to ask his friends for ideas.

    c. Other:

L: Look at the solutions again and choose one.

Which solution would help you learn to share?

V: Validate the solution by trying it.

Practice each possible solution as you role-play with your classmates.

E: Evaluate how the solution worked.

If the solution did not solve the problem, return to step **S** and see if any other solutions might work. Continue with the steps.

Extended Learning Activities

1. Problem-Solving Practice Scenario

> Imagine you are walking in line and you trip and fall down. You are not hurt, but some other students laugh. What would you do?

I: Identify the problem.

> ➤ Kids laughed when you tripped and fell down.

S: Solutions to the problem?

    a. Laugh out loud, too, and say, "I don't know how that happened."

    b. Ignore the other kids laughing.

    c. Other:

O: Obstacles to the solutions?

    a. It might be difficult to laugh at yourself if your feelings are hurt.

    b. Ignoring the other kids is hard to do when your feelings are hurt.

    c. Other:

L: Look at the solutions again and choose one.

Choose the solution that would solve the problem without violence.

V: Validate the solution by trying it.

Practice each possible solution as you role-play with your classmates.

E: Evaluate how the solution worked.

If your first solution did not work, then return to step **S** and review the remaining solutions.

2. Reinforcement Activity

Give each student a copy of the "Frustrated Franklin" reinforcement activity. Explain that Franklin felt frustrated in the book because his friends would not play with him as long as he did not share decisions about which games to play. Tell students to write a letter to Franklin with their advice about how to solve the problem.

Frustrated Franklin

Directions: Write a letter to Franklin giving him your advice about how to solve his problem.

_____

_____

_____

_____

_____

_____

_____

_____

_____

_____

_____

_____

The Greedy Triangle

Title: *The Greedy Triangle*
Author: Marilyn Burns
Copyright: 1994
Publisher: Scholastic
ISBN: 0-590-48991-7
Topic: Self-acceptance
Approximate Grade Levels: 1–3

Book Summary:

> The triangle is not happy with its shape, so it goes to the local shape-shifter to add more lines and angles. After the excitement of each new shape wears off, the triangle tries another shape until it realizes being a triangle is best of all.

Lesson Goal:

> To help students recognize that we should not be selfish about the way we look and to accept and enjoy ourselves.

Prereading Activities:

> Ask students to look around the classroom and name some items shaped like a triangle. Point out that many things are shaped like a triangle. Tell them today's book is about a triangle who does not like its shape. Ask students to predict why the triangle does not like its shape.

During Reading:

> Read the book aloud. Before revealing if the triangle decided to remain a triangle, stop and use the I SOLVE strategy to predict potential solutions. Discuss the story using the discussion questions if applicable.

Postreading/Discussion Questions:

1. What are most triangles busy doing?
2. Where did the triangle like being best?
3. Can you make the triangle's favorite spot?
4. Why was the triangle feeling dissatisfied?
5. Who is the shape-shifter?
6. Why did the triangle, even as a new shape, become dissatisfied?
7. What shape did the triangle turn into?
8. Why did the shape's friends avoid it?
9. What made the shape finally say, "Enough"?
10. How did the triangle's friends feel when it was back to being a triangle again?

I SOLVE Strategy

I: Identify the problem presented in the book.

➤ The triangle is not happy being a triangle.

S: Solutions to the problem?

    a. Book solution: The triangle went to the shape-shifter and tried being many different shapes.

    b. If the triangle was dissatisfied with its shape, it could have talked to a friend or family member about the problem.

    c. Other:

O: Obstacles to the solutions?

    a. Book solution: As humans, we cannot go to a shape-shifter and change the way we look without a lot of pain and surgery.

    b. Talking to a friend could have helped the triangle unless the triangle could not find a friend to talk with.

    c. Other:

L: Look at the solutions again and choose one.

Which one could help you feel better about yourself?

V: Validate the solution by trying it.

Practice each possible solution as you role-play with your classmates.

E: Evaluate how the solution worked.

Remember to choose a solution that will help you feel good about yourself as well as solve the problem. If the solution did not solve the problem, return to step **S** and see if any other solutions might work. Continue with the steps.

Extended Learning Activities

1. Problem-Solving Practice Scenario

Imagine you just got an ice-cream cone, and as you are walking away from the counter, the ice cream falls off the cone and onto the floor. What would you do?

I: Identify the problem.

> ➤ Your ice cream fell off the cone as soon as you walked away from the ice-cream store counter.

S: Solutions to the problem?

    a.   Return to the counter and tell the employee what happened.

    b.   Say to yourself, "This was an accident. I won't get mad."

    c.   Other:

O: Obstacles to the solutions?

    a.   The employee at the ice-cream shop could say, "Sorry, there is nothing we can do about it."

    b.   You may feel too upset to say to yourself, "This was an accident. I won't get mad."

    c.   Other:

L: Look at the solutions again and choose one.

Choose the solution that would solve the problem and get you a new ice-cream cone.

V: Validate the solution by trying it.

Practice each possible solution as you role-play with your classmates.

E: Evaluate how the solution worked.

Which solution would help you get a new ice-cream cone? If the solution does not work, return to step **S** and review the remaining solutions.

2.   Reinforcement Activity

Give each student a copy of "Perplexing Polygons." Review the names of each polygon based on its number of sides. Ask students to draw an example of each polygon. Students can also create a story about their favorite polygon shape.

Perplexing Polygons

Directions: A polygon is named for the number of sides it has. Read the names of each polygon with your teacher. Draw an example of each shape. Which shape is your favorite? Write a story about your favorite shape.

3 sides = triangle

4 sides = quadrilateral

5 sides = pentagon

6 sides = hexagon

7 sides = heptagon

8 sides = octagon

9 sides = nonagon

10 sides = decagon

11 sides = undecagon

12 sides = dodecagon

Draw an example of each shape below (use extra paper if needed):

Additional Readings on Selfishness and Sharing

Title and Author: *The Berenstain Bears Lend a Helping Hand* by Stan and
  Jan Berenstain
ISBN: 0-679-88956-6
Approximate Grade Levels: K–3
Copyright: 1998

Book Summary:
  The bear cubs learn to think about others when they help an elderly neighbor clean out her attic.

Title and Author: *Crabby Gabby* by Stephen Cosgrove
ISBN: 0-843-11441-X
Approximate Grade Levels: K–3
Copyright: 1986

Book Summary:
  Gabby's friends become tired of her demands and refuse to play with her. Gabby runs off by her-
  self, where she receives the advice that games are not just for winning but for enjoyment, too.
  Gabby learns to share with her friends and stop being selfish.

Title and Author: *Jared and the Ordinary, Handy-Dandy, Excellent,*
  Extraordinary Plain Brown String: A Story About the Joy of Sharing
  by Dana Webb
ISBN: 0-781-43052-6
Approximate Grade Levels: K–3
Copyright: 1999

Book Summary:
  Jared and his sister are challenged by their parents to see how many things they can do with some
  leftover wrapping paper. Jared learns about sharing as he helps others with his brown string.

Author/Title Index

Subject Index

About the Author

James W. Forgan, Ph.D., is an Assistant Professor of Special Education at Florida Atlantic University where he teaches undergraduate and graduate courses and is the principal investigator on several funded grants. He was a teacher of students with learning disabilities and behavior disorders at the elementary and middle school level for six years in the Miami-Dade County Public Schools. His professional interests are in social skills instruction for all students, including those with mild disabilities.

Contact James Forgan at Florida Atlantic University, 5353 Parkside Drive, Jupiter, FL 33458. *E-mail*: jforgan@fau.edu.